Teaching Library Skills for Academic Credit

by Mignon S. Adams
and Jacquelyn M. Morris

ORYX PRESS
1985

The rare Arabian Oryx is believed to have inspired the myth of the unicorn. This desert antelope became virtually extinct in the early 1960s. At that time several groups of international conservationists arranged to have 9 animals sent to the Phoenix Zoo to be the nucleus of a captive breeding herd. Today the Oryx population is over 400 and herds have been returned to reserves in Israel, Jordan, and Oman.

Copyright © 1985 by
The Oryx Press
2214 North Central at Encanto
Phoenix, Arizona 85004-1483
Published simultaneously in Canada

Printed and Bound in the United States of America

Library of Congress Cataloging in Publication Data

Adams, Mignon S.
  Teaching library skills for academic credit.

  Bibliography: p.
  Includes index.
    1. Libraries, University and college.   2. College
students—Library orientation.   3. Bibliography—
Methodology—Study and teaching (Higher)   4. Libraries
and education.   I. Morris, Jacquelyn M.   II. Title.
Z675.U5A413   1985   025.5'677   83-43238
ISBN 0-89774-138-2

"To our husbands"

Contents

Preface

Over the past 15 years, bibliographic instruction—the teaching of students to use a library effectively—has become a part of the role of most academic libraries in the United States. Teaching library skills for academic credit is a particular type of bibliographic instruction, a type which may take the form of a separate library course or as an important part of another course. When students receive credit for the learning of library skills, they also learn that the ability to use a library is part of their academic training.

Credit library instruction is widespread. Carolyn Kirkendall, director of LOEX, the national clearinghouse for library use instruction, reports that she receives each year more and more requests for materials on library courses. Over the past several years, the requests have been increasingly concerned with ways to connect course content to students' curricula.

The purpose of this book is to offer, in one place, a detailed guide for the development and maintenance of a library course, with information ranging from how to survive politically to how to use an overhead projector. The last half of this book describes courses from all over the country—courses which reflect different levels and approaches. While this book contains information which may be of value to any teaching librarian, it is not intended to be a general introduction to the field of bibliographic instruction. Other excellent books exist for that purpose; the authors particularly recommend *Learning the Library,* by Anne Beaubien, Mary George, and Sharon Hogan (New York: Bowker, 1983).

The authors have a combined experience of 14 years in teaching library skills for academic credit. It is our hope that what we have learned through trial and error, through attending conferences, and through corresponding with colleagues also teaching courses, will be of use to others involved in credit library instruction.

Mignon S. Adams
Coordinator of Information Services
Penfield Library
State University of New York at Oswego
Jacquelyn M. Morris
Associate Dean of Libraries
University of the Pacific

Acknowledgements

We would like to extend our thanks to the following people:

Sylvia Bender-Lamb, University of the Pacific, for her thoroughness in surveying the literature on credit courses and her careful preparation of the bibliography

Jennifer Cargill and Brian Alley, Oryx Press, for their encouragement and early support

Carolyn Kirkendall, Project LOEX, for her advice, encouragement, and prompt response to our every request for help and materials

Patricia O. Robinson, State University of New York at Oswego, for her careful reading of every word of the manuscript, despite being uninterested in the subject

All of the writers of case studies that appear in this book, both for their willingness to contribute and their timely delivery—and for their contributions, which we found to be well-written and thought-provoking

Our husbands for their patience and unflagging support.

Teaching Library Skills for Academic Credit

Part I: Theory and Practice

Chapter 1:
The Library Course: What and Why

There are a variety of approaches to teaching library skills. As a growing body of literature shows, library usage has been taught in the format of one or 2 sessions of a regular course (course-related sessions), tours, term paper clinics, and other orientations. An approach that appears frequently in the literature is the library credit course—the teaching of library skills within the framework of a course when all or a significant portion of the course is under the direction and control of a librarian.

But if library skills can be taught in other ways, why should they be taught for credit? Giving academic credit is the way in which higher education legitimizes learning; the way by which students are told that certain skills and knowledge are important. By allowing a course to be given for credit, the college faculty is tacitly approving the content of a course. Moreover, in our system of higher education, tangible awards such as credit and grades are the recognized ways of motivating students. Like writing and mathematical skills, library skills are essential tools for learning, ones which students would like to have but will probably not work to attain unless there is some built-in extrinsic motivation to do so. While receiving credit is not necessary for learning these basic skills, granting credit provides the extrinsic motivation needed by many students.

Aside from credit, a course format offers other advantages. Foremost is the time available for instruction. A course allows time for a structured and comprehensive approach toward learning. Students have time to develop search strategies, to explore alternative approaches, and to practice information-seeking behavior under controlled circumstances until both the instructor and the student feel confident that the goals of the course have been achieved.

Students like what they gain from library courses. They appreciate learning skills which they can put to immediate use. In the case studies contained in the second half of this book are several references to how much the students feel they learn from library courses. Elective courses succeed because students tell other students that the library course is beneficial.

Another advantage of a credit course is its relative autonomy. Most credit courses are not dependent upon maintaining a relationship with a department or individual faculty members. Many library instruction programs designed with the full cooperation and involvement of a library-oriented faculty member die when that person leaves the university.

Librarians also like what they gain from credit courses. Most of the contacts librarians usually have with students are anonymous. A course allows librarians to get to know individual students and to develop a professional relationship with them. The feedback most librarians receive when they teach library courses is generally positive; their belief is reinforced that libraries and library skills are important. And, of course, teaching a credit course helps to substantiate the role of the librarian as a full member of the educational mission.

Some arguments are made against library courses. One argument—that library courses are boring and meaningless—is disproved constantly by the students who take such courses. Another argument sometimes heard is that it is inappropriate for librarians to teach. Since academic librarians have been busily teaching for the past 15 years, this argument hardly merits attention.

The most-often expressed disagreement is that courses take too much time for the number of students they reach. Courses do indeed take time; many services in libraries take a great deal of time. However, courses have an impact on individual students which other library services may not.

Under what circumstances should a library consider offering a course? Librarians at some institutions have opted to offer a course when they want to ensure that all students meet a basic level of competency, without the library having to depend on the cooperation of one department (or when there has been no department which reaches all students). Other librarians have responded to the desire on the part of some students to obtain advanced library skills. At other institutions, members of a library science or educational media department have seen a library use course as one which can attract students and increase enrollment in their departments. Many librarians have been willing to devote extra time and energy to developing and teaching a course because of the very real benefits they receive from doing so.

WHAT IS A LIBRARY COURSE?

Library usage has been taught for credit in many different ways; there is no standard format. Some courses are 3- or 4-credit courses, open as electives to anyone on campus. Others are planned for particular majors and are taken in conjunction with another academic course. Many are one or 2 credits. The audience may range from freshmen to graduate students. The case studies in the last portion of this book illustrate some possible ways to teach library skills for credit; many approaches can work successfully.

In choosing a format, you must be guided as much by what is possible and politically feasible at your institution as by your personal preference. A course radically different in length or format from other courses on campus may not fit into students' schedules. Others on campus may not agree with your concept. However, keeping your particular institution in mind, you may choose from among a variety of different formats.

LOWER-LEVEL VERSUS UPPER-LEVEL

The most logical point to offer a library course often seems to be at a freshman level. This is the year when many skills courses—such as writing courses, introductory mathematics, and computer programing—are taught. Since most students need library skills for their entire college career, learning about the library early on gives them a head start. Most students come to college with little research experience and even those lucky enough to have been taught library or research skills are not prepared for the complex organization and advanced materials in a college or university library. These students are also the ones who make heavy demands on the reference desk, requiring librarians to teach basic skills on a one-to-one basis, over and over again. For these reasons, many institutions have chosen to place their library course at the freshman level.

However, other librarians feel courses are more beneficial if they are offered at a later point in the student's college career. Instructors of library use at the freshman level face the same problems as do the teachers of freshman composition: students neither realize what they don't know nor what they need to know, and they do not yet, in many cases, have any real need for library skills in other courses. Many college freshmen can barely read professional literature, let alone appreciate the skills needed to locate it.

Sophomores and juniors are usually well into their majors and have often had some frustrating experiences in locating information for research projects. They therefore see a real need for what they're learning and can apply it almost immediately. Their motivation and interest in the class tend to be much higher than that of freshmen. Factors to be considered in selecting a level include the following:

1. Is the course to be a basic skills course, or is it intended to teach advanced tools required for a major?
2. Are basic skills already well-covered through an active bibliographic instruction program which reaches most freshmen? Or, does the course-related program primarily reach only upper-level majors? The credit course needs to fit in with the overall bibliographic instruction program.
3. Are there supportive faculty members who see the course as beneficial to their students and who will advise them to take it? For what level do they see the course as appropriate?
4. Do the students have freer schedules as freshmen or upper-level students? Some institutions have stringent general education requirements which leave little room in the *first* 2 years of a student's curriculum for other courses, while other college programs have many requirements for some majors during their last 2 years. Deans or a student advisement center can usually supply this answer.

Courses have been taught successfully for freshmen through graduate students. The right level for a particular course depends upon the structure of the institution, needs of the students, and the nature of an already existing instruction program.

REQUIRED OR ELECTIVE

Many institutions have chosen to concentrate their library instructional efforts on a course which is required for all students. There are many reasons for doing so. Librarians can ensure that all students have basic competency in library skills. The success of the course is not dependent upon the 2-way relationship of one librarian or library program with one faculty member or discipline. The course may be highly visible on campus and may, therefore, be able to draw upon financial and internal support it might not otherwise have. Required courses have been developed which serve large numbers of students; for example, 3,000 students are enrolled each semester in a half-credit course at Iowa State University (see Case Study #3). While offering a required course for all students demands a large commitment of staff time and resources, libraries which have done so feel that the commitment, resulting in better and more extensive library use, is well worth it.

Library courses may also be required for certain majors. These courses will not demand the large amount of resources that one for all students will, and there is an opportunity to tailor the class to meet student needs more specifically. Unfortunately, a common occurrence is that a college academic department decides to include an already established library course as a requirement for a major, without informing the library staff of it until the requirement is already on the books. The staff is then faced with a commitment before it has decided to accept it.

Required courses provide a steady audience; little or no marketing is necessary. Librarians can also feel assured that all students, or at least all of some majors, meet a standard level of competency. However, in addition to the commitment that must be made by the staff, required courses generate some other problems.

Decisions on requirements are not made by the library, but by individual departments, or, in the case of all-campus requirements, by faculty committees. Changes in requirements can be made with little or no library input. If supportive people leave the institution, the library may find its course—to which it has committed time, money, and staff—questioned as a requirement. Therefore, campus support must be monitored and maintained.

Another problem with required courses is that students never seem to like a course they must take so much as one they choose.

Campuswide student rating scales often have separate norms for required courses, because their general rating is consistently lower. Because they may see no need for it, students may resent having to take a library course more than other required courses. The instructor will need to prove the worth of the course, using such methods as administering a difficult pretest (to demonstrate to students that they do not know so much as they think they do) or by giving copious illustrations of ways in which the course will be beneficial.

The students in elective courses are generally more motivated. Students who find the course not to their liking have the freedom to drop it (just as the instructor has the freedom to encourage students whose enthusiasm is low or who do not meet the prerequisites to drop it). However, some librarians have found enrollment to be consistently low in elective courses. It can take a longer time for an elective course to become established, and an elective course will never reach the number of students that a required one will. Required courses need to be sold to the students already enrolled in them; electives need to be sold consistently and continually, both to faculty advisors and to students.

SPONSORSHIP

Through what department will the course be taught? This is a political decision, because the sponsoring department then receives credit for the students. This credit is usually expressed in terms of FTE's—full time equivalency—which is obtained by multiplying the number of credits for the course by the number of students enrolled in the course and dividing this number by the number of credits considered a normal student load. Funding and staffing decisions are often made on the basis of FTE's and the number of FTE's generated per instructor. A class with a large enrollment thus supports the department's ability to offer classes with small enrollments as well.

In many institutions, the library is not considered to be a faculty department and therefore cannot sponsor courses itself. Where existing, a library school or an undergraduate media or library science department may be a logical choice for sponsorship. In a number of colleges, an undergraduate library-use course has helped to support library and/or media departments which have declining enrollments. It is ironic that the argument that library classes take too much staff time becomes an asset when the course is part of such a department.

If there is no library/media department, another academic department may be a logical choice. For basic courses, the English department may be the best choice, while for upper-level subject courses, another department may be more appropriate. The FTE's generated by the course will then go to the sponsoring department, which is an attractive prospect, since the department does not have to average the librarian in as one of its instructors. If the library has no need for FTE's for funding or staffing support, then it may be politically astute to let another department accumulate them.

As an alternative, there may be at the institution some catch-all designation, such as "general studies," which can be used for courses which do not fit into a specific department. The FTE's generated may be accumulated by the library or they may go into an all-campus pool. Finally, many colleges have numbers for newly created or innovative courses. Frequently these numbers allow a course to be taught for one or 2 semesters to determine interest or to find an audience. More than one bibliographic instruction course has begun on this basis.

In the second half of this book, case studies illustrate the various ways in which courses have been sponsored. Some of these illustrations reflect interesting patterns of evolution.

DEPENDENT COURSES

Some libraries have solved the problem of course sponsorship by "piggybacking" the library course onto another course; for a basic skills course, this could mean an English composition class. Students might be required to take an additional one-credit library course if they take the other class, or students may elect to take it as an addition.

The relationship between the 2 courses may vary. In some instances, the classes may be closely integrated with the assignments for the library course designed to coordinate with the assignments for the other. Or, the relationship may be purely administrative (see "Case Study #1: Central Oregon Community College" for an example of a course which has evolved to be curricularly separate from the composition course to which it is attached).

Another approach is to include a significant library component in an already-established course. "Case Study #15: Mankato State University" is an example of this approach. It describes a required sociology course for corrections majors in which a librarian conducts one-fourth of the course and gives library assignments. The course remains a sociology course and the final evaluation is done by the instructor from the sociology department.

Dependent courses can obviate many administrative problems for the library. In addition, if the coordination between the instructors is close, and students can clearly see the application of the library component to the rest of the class, they may be more highly motivated. However, like traditional course-related library instruction, the success of such a course depends on a good working relationship between the 2 instructors. If one of them leaves the institution, the course may wither and die.

ONLY GENERAL, OR COURSE-RELATED TOO?

Many library courses are general in nature, with all students, regardless of major, completing the same requirements. When there are large numbers of students, a general course may be necessary simply to cope with developing and grading of assignments. Freshman-level courses, taught to students before they become oriented to their majors, will probably be more general than upper-level courses. However, the more general the course, the more difficult it is to make it relevant to individual students. Student motivation and enthusiasm will be higher if they can see a direct relationship between the course materials and their own information needs.

Even a general course can be developed to take advantage of individual students' needs and interests. For example, if the course is planned for freshmen on a campus which requires a freshman composition class, the librarian may devise assignments which relate to writing assignments of the composition class. Or, students might be encouraged to take, at the same time, another course which requires the completion of a research paper or project, whose topic can be the subject of the library assignments. If the library course is planned for certain majors (political science or chemistry, for example), then the library assignments can be designed to fit the information needs of these majors.

The more closely related the library course is to other course work, the greater the motivation and enthusiasm of the students is likely to be. While librarians view the acquisition of library skills to be valuable in itself, students seldom do if they cannot immediately recognize their application.

INDEPENDENT STUDY

Many library courses have been taught by having students work independently, or almost independently, usually with some type of workbook. An independent study course is often viewed as requiring the least amount of time and effort on the part of the library staff. The number of students in a semester may vary from a few to hundreds. For required courses reaching a large number of students, this approach may be the most feasible.

There are some drawbacks to an independent study format. Many students lack the self-motivation to work completely independently on assignments. Such courses traditionally generate a large number of incompletes. In addition, it is difficult to create assignments which can be done completely independently that teach more than the use of tools (although that may be all that is desired).

Another drawback is that it often takes far more time than expected to create assignments, have them reproduced, and score them. If multiple-choice or standard answer worksheets are used and graded, a number of different versions must be developed in order to guard against students merely copying others' work. Also, libraries change, so worksheets must be revised periodically. Many bibliographic instruction librarians would rather spend time in a classroom than updating and revising worksheets.

These drawbacks can be mitigated in several ways. Meeting a few times, even in a large group, provides more motivation to students. Making (and keeping) strict deadlines for each assignment encourages students to avoid falling behind. If the worksheets are ungraded and students held responsible only for taking and passing examinations over the material, then only one version of the worksheets needs to be done. There are also some commercial materials available, such as the *Materials and Methods for...* series (Neal-Schuman), in which multiple assignments and answer sheets have already been created. Finally, using computers or media may be an option.

Computer Use

Computers can be an enormous help. Most institutions have a standard grading package, so that if answers to a worksheet are recorded on a machine-readable form, scoring time is minimal. In addition, a microcomputer can be programed to generate the worksheets. For example, if a worksheet has 10 questions, there can be several—say 3—different versions of each question. The micro can be instructed to pick one version for each question and print out 30 different worksheets (a far simpler procedure than manually preparing 30 different pieces of paper).

Computer-Assisted Instruction (CAI)

One solution for independent study courses is to place the entire course on a computer, which can administer the worksheets, keep track of scores, and test students. This solution is viable only if the institution is willing to commit a large amount of resources to developing and programing the course materials. Over the next few years, however, college-level bibliographic instruction software should become commercially available, which should make computer-assisted library instruction possible for many institutions.

Media Use

Instruction by media is an option for independent study classes. Videocassettes or slide/tapes can be set up for students to view when they wish (audio-only cassettes should be avoided; only automobile commuters are willing to listen to an hour's worth of instruction). Like CAI, effective audiovisual materials require a great deal of time to prepare, but many institutions provide photographic and other support services more generously than programing support.

Independent study courses should be considered an option when there are large numbers of students to instruct and the library has insufficient personnel. The courses will work best (and result in fewer student incompletes) if they are required or part of the requirements for another course so that the students have extensive motivation to finish them. The option of an elective course for independent study is a nice one to have available for the few mature students who like to learn on their own and who are self-motivated enough to finish. There must be, however, sufficient time and resources for developing the materials and also the realization that students will seldom be as enthusiastic about them as about courses taught in other ways.

NUMBER OF HOURS

Most library courses tend to carry credit of one or 2 hours. When a librarian first begins to plan a course, it often seems difficult to conceive enough activities to fill even one hour's credit. However, it seems that, over a period of several semesters, the librarian will initiate an increasing number, until one hour seems confining. At this point, some librarians then expand the course to 2 hours or investigate offering a more advanced course.

There is some feeling that the more credit hours a course bears, the more serious the subject matter. On most campuses, one-hour courses tend to be physical education service courses, while 5-hour courses are most likely in the sciences. Because of this, student expectations of a one- or 2-credit course sometimes are that it should have little outside work and certainly not have the requirements of a "real" course.

Be that as it may, librarians may have an easier time gaining the approval of library administrators and faculty committees if the course is one or 2 credits. The library administrator will view it as requiring less time and commitment and faculty committees, who may view the course as remedial, may be less adamant in their opposition since the course offers "only" one or 2 credits.

Courses have been taught successfully as even half-credit courses. Again, you must determine what is most feasible at your institution. In many cases, it might be most desirable to begin with a one- or 2-hour course, and, after the course is well-established, investigate increasing the hours.

CONFIGURATION

Library courses may, like most courses, meet the same number of times per week as the credit they carry for the entire semester or quarter. However, many library courses are configured differently. Often, courses meet for a double block of time. That is, a 2-credit course may meet for 2 hours once a week rather than one hour twice a week. Librarians who choose this format like it because it allows both for class discussion and for the students to work in the library with the librarian immediately available. A cautionary note: unless it is made very clear to students that they are expected to remain for the whole period, they may disappear, mumbling that they'll do the assignment later (and undoubtedly poorly). Meeting back in the classroom at the end for a few minutes' discussion on the assignment can solve this problem.

Another variation is to have the library course meet for the first half or so of the term. For classes in which students are encouraged to use topics from other courses for their library assignments, this format allows them to have the research component of their papers done by mid-term, leaving the rest of the term for them to write them. In situations where the librarian has other public service duties, such as reference or online searching, this format also has the advantage of finishing at midterm, usually a time when the library is becoming much more busy and demanding for the librarian.

Some libraries also offer courses for less than the term so that several classes can be taught during the term. A disadvantage is that students who begin a course near the end of a semester often feel so pressured by the work from other classes that they may give the library course short shrift.

There are some definite advantages to experimenting with different configurations. However, designing an unusual format cannot be done in a vacuum. A 2-hour format which keeps students from taking another class either before or after the library course will probably not succeed. Again, check with someone who is heavily involved with scheduling and advisement to see if an unusual configuration will work at your institution.

LOOKING AHEAD

There are a variety of formats in which library credit courses have been taught and each has strengths and weaknesses. However, there are many other considerations involved in planning a credit course. How does a course become established? How do you get a course off the drawing board and into the classroom?

How do you know when you're succeeding? The rest of this book deals with these and other issues related to the development of a course.

Chapter 2 outlines the political realities that many librarians have found to exist when attempting to add this method of instruction to their bibliographic instruction program. Like any real-life situation, political pressures may torpedo a new venture without the initiator even realizing they existed.

Chapter 3 deals with planning a course, including goal definition and developing an outline. Some common approaches to organizing a course are reviewed.

Developing assignments and materials for teaching a course can be time-consuming. Methods of approach and practical suggestions are covered in Chapter 4.

What is effective teaching, and how can a librarian go about improving teaching techniques? Chapter 5 reviews the research on effective teaching and gives practical advice on improving what occurs in the classroom.

Whether you have succeeded and whether the time and effort were worthwhile are things you want to know—and most assuredly others do also. Testing the objectives of the course, using various instruments, and disseminating the results are discussed in Chapter 6.

Finally, the last section of this book presents case studies of courses taught at institutions around the country. While some have been more successful than others, all give examples and ideas of ways to approach teaching library courses. A bibliography, resource list, and an appendix containing teaching tips round out this book.

REFERENCE

Materials and Methods for... New York: Neal-Schuman.

FOR FURTHER READING

Renford, B., and Hendrickson, L. (1980). *Bibliographic instruction: A handbook.* New York: Neal-Schuman.
Chapter 5 contains a detailed discussion of the mechanics of setting up a workbook program for a large number of students.

Chapter 2:
Establishing the Library Course

So you want to teach a library course. College librarians are seldom in a position to be able to offer a course solely on their own initiative. Rather, they must work with others and within a structure. The library director must be convinced, the support of other librarians is needed, the course must go through the usual campus procedures for curricular additions, and students must be attracted to it. After the course is established, it must be maintained. Many library courses have failed, either because of low enrollment or other college pressures. Overcoming some of these hurdles while avoiding pitfalls is the subject of this chapter.

GAINING THE SUPPORT OF THE LIBRARY ADMINISTRATOR

Some courses have been initiated by a library director. In other cases, library directors have been immediately supportive of librarian efforts. However, in most cases, at least some selling must be done in order to gain the full support of the library administration.

The director is the person who has to decide where scarce resources are to be allocated. For good reason, s/he will be cautious about committing staff time and resources to new activities without a clear understanding of costs and benefits. Consequently, there should be a great deal of informal discussion first, long before a planned course package is presented for the director's approval. Discussion should involve not only the director, but other librarians as well. It should make clear how a library course fits into the overall goals of the library.

On the other hand, the director is interested in activities which will promote the use of the library, will make him/her look effective, and which will involve ideas that other libraries have found to be successful. The director will want to feel that those who propose the course are enthusiastically committed to it and have the abilities to carry it out. These are the points you will want to address.

Major objections a director will have are the time required from a staff which probably already views itself as overburdened and resistance from other librarians. If time is diverted to teaching a library course, what other services will suffer? What can be given up?

How much time does a library course take? A one-hour course will meet for probably 14 to 16 hours during a semester. Time spent outside class will vary a great deal, depending on the teaching experience of the librarian and the amount of grading time required. Some experienced librarians, teaching a class they have taught before, feel that 2 to 3 hours of outside time for each class hour is sufficient. Other librarians may require closer to 5 hours and certainly the first time a class is taught, developing the materials will take a great deal of time.

Library instruction is a recent addition to library services. Seldom are traditional library services examined to see if they merit the time spent on them. Perhaps your library provides reference service from 8 a.m. to 9 a.m. on weekdays. Probably few reference questions are answered during this time period, yet this service can add up to over 250 hours per year. This is more than the amount of time required to teach a one-hour course for 2 semesters, yet a course will have a far greater impact than those 250 hours.

Starting on a small scale may relieve some of the fears of overcommitment. A one- or 2-credit course offered for only one section on a trial basis may demonstrate that a course is possible given the present level of staffing. It may also be possible to teach the course as extra service. Many campuses have available funds to pay instructors for overloads. If such funds are available and you are willing to extend your workday, then the argument of staff time becomes moot.

The other major drawback the director will see is the resistance of other librarians. Those who are not involved in the course may feel that they may be asked to pick up the slack or that their work is being viewed as unimportant. They are the ones who are likely to voice feelings that teaching is inappropriate for librarians or that the course will reach too few students to be justifiable. It is important to make the effort from the beginning to involve as many other librarians as possible. Ask for their input as to what a course should include. Plan to incorporate their ideas and their expertise into the actual teaching of the course.

The director will also be concerned about other costs: space, secretarial help, equipment, and supplies. Space may be a particular problem. Be willing if necessary to meet outside the library if there is no way to obtain suitable space without displacing others (not a politically wise move). Start modestly with requests for equipment and supplies. Once the course is up and running, you'll have a much better idea of what is necessary and what is merely nice. The need for secretarial help may be met by student workers or by having class materials prepared during slow times (summer or between semesters). Find out the level of secretarial help received by other instructors on campus. You may find that they grade their own exams, type and duplicate their own materials, clean their own chalkboards. Do not expect more than they have.

Once the director has made a commitment to a library course, s/he should be asked to gather support from deans or other campus administrators. It is the director who can make the best case for such a course.

CAMPUS SUPPORT

Once support from the library is ensured, then support from others on campus becomes necessary. For a required course, this step will involve a great deal of work. The library cannot set requirements itself. Some required library courses have been instituted as part of an overall change in general education. Others have become requirements after the course has been taught for awhile and its worth has been demonstrated. Generally, campus-required courses have been developed because a high-level college administrator has been interested and supportive. Courses for a particular major have generally become requirements through the interest of individual faculty members or department chairs.

Informal contacts are extremely important. Many courses begin through informal discussion with administrators or faculty members. Garnering this support is essential both for establishing the course and for ensuring its survival. If there is already an active library instruction program, the best place to find faculty support is through those who are enthusiastic participants in the course-related program.

Once you have established that there is interest among administrators and faculty, then it is time to investigate the formal process of course approval. This is a process with which librarians are often unfamiliar. Like any academic process, it can be politically charged, so it is to your advantage to be fully informed. Talk to department chairs and administrators about what problems can arise. If the course is to be sponsored by the library and the library has never sponsored a course before, make sure that this is possible. Otherwise, you should probably seek out another department to sponsor the course, at least on a temporary basis. Many departments have a course number reserved for experimental or topics courses which allows for a course to be taught for a limited time period without formal approval.

On many campuses, proposed new courses must be approved by a campus or divisional committee. Find out who the chair and its members are. Identify someone on the committee who is supportive of library use and talk through your course idea with him/her. Ask what kinds of problems may come up in the process of getting course approval from the committee and ask for any guidelines the committee might have. Generally, you will be asked to submit a course proposal for the approval process, the format of which will vary from campus to campus. Follow guidelines and the committee member's suggestions exactly. Arguments that faculty members often raise about library credit courses are these:

- The course is remedial and therefore should not carry credit.
- The course is a skills course and has no content.
- Other faculty members, not librarians, should be teaching research methods.
- The course is just not appropriate.
- If librarians teach a course, then all other personnel, such as counselors and nurses, will want to teach courses as well.

Be prepared to counter these arguments with your course proposal and include some documentation. One of the strongest points that can be made is that library credit courses are taught at many different colleges (the one at the University of California–Berkeley, for example, is over 15 years old, and few would argue that Berkeley is academically deficient). Include a list of colleges which offer courses and state the prerequisites for the course, which should include skills that entering freshmen should bring with them from high school. Demonstrate that you are teaching more advanced skills. If any testing of library skills has been done with your college's students, include the results to indicate that students need the course. Compare the library course with other skills-type courses: English composition, computer programing, research methods. Ask several faculty members to write letters indicating their support of such a program, giving reasons why they favor it.

A typically unvoiced concern, but a very real one, is that every new course necessarily diverts students from other courses; their selection of one course means that there will be another course they do not take. However, if the proposed course is only one or 2 credits, then faculty members may not see it as threatening to their courses.

Your very best support will be a convinced committee member, one who can personally counter arguments. Some librarians have actually waited until there is such a person on the committee or have even (in institutions where librarians have full faculty status) worked toward the election or appointment of a librarian to the committee.

If you have done the appropriate groundwork in gathering support and documentation, then approval by the faculty curriculum committee will probably not be too difficult.

MARKETING THE COURSE

An elective course must have students. When the course is new, it is certainly not enough to have it listed in the schedule of course offerings. Some kinds of marketing techniques must be used. It is also wise to start small; it's better to have to turn away students during the first semester than to have several half-filled sections.

Faculty Contacts

Faculty advisors are one of the most valuable sources for student enrollment. Those faculty members who originally supported the course will be likely candidates to send you students, as well as those who have participated in course-related instruction. Inform other faculty about the course. Make sure that it's clear what kind of students will profit from the class; if it's not intended to be remedial, explain why not. Some methods used by librarians to inform faculty have been these:

- Announcements or presentations made at general faculty or departmental meetings.
- Flyers sent out to faculty members or advisement coordinators.
- Articles placed in a library or campus newsletter.

If the course is aimed at freshmen, then find out how freshmen are advised. Many campuses hold special summer advisement and orientation sessions for incoming freshmen. It may be possible to talk to advisors in a group before the summer program begins or to prepare materials to go into advisement packets.

Advertising

On some campuses, courses are routinely advertised. Such advertising may take the form of flyers posted around campus or an announcement printed in the college newspaper. One enterprising librarian took advantage of his paper's personal column to insert messages ("Lori: Remember the rough time you had finding info for your paper last semester? Don't forget to sign up for LIB 200 and learn how to do it the right way.)

Another good place to advertise is in the library itself. A display or posters about the course may be especially effective at preregistration time, which is often the same time that students are feeling panicky about the papers they've been researching that semester.

Remember in your advertising to stress the benefits the students will get from the course. These are likely to be that they will feel proficient and confident in the library and that they will be able to write better papers. Some librarians leave at the reference or reserve desk a packet of explanatory materials, including copies of the syllabus and assignments.

The course can also be described in course-related instruction and at general library orientations and tours. Faculty members who are supportive of library courses are often glad to announce them and encourage student enrollment.

Naturally, a required course will have no difficulty attracting students. However, you may still want to do some marketing. Providing some information about the class may help to shape student expectations and reinforce the fact that the course will cover information that is both new and helpful. A one-page flyer in new student packets could describe these benefits; a story in the campus newspaper can emphasize why the course was started and what it was meant to accomplish.

Once the course is established, much of the enrollment may come from word-of-mouth. Even so, it is important to maintain and refresh contacts with faculty advisors and to continue marketing the course to future students.

SURVIVING

Many library courses have not survived. They go out of existence because student enrollment is low, or because key administrative support is lost, or because other librarians are not in favor of the course. Once a course is established, it is important to monitor and respond to student needs and to ensure that the course has high visibility.

Maintaining Student Enrollment

Some factors over which the librarian has little control may affect student enrollment. New general education requirements may mean that students no longer have enough flexibility in their schedules to take the course. Faculty members may require fewer research papers and projects, which means that students will see less need for using the library. Other forms of library instruction may be so effective that students feel no need to take another course. However, most enrollment declines occur when the librarian in charge fails to monitor why students enroll in the course and fails to ensure that the course fits their needs.

Always ask in class (this can be part of the background information you ask for in class, along with student telephone numbers) how students heard about the course. Depending upon your institution, typical replies are likely to be "from a friend," "from my advisor," "from the course schedule," or "I saw a notice on a bulletin board." Note the general trend of these replies and be sensitive if any category begins to decline.

Many courses succeed primarily by word-of-mouth among students. If students regard the course as a "good" one and one from which they gained a great deal, they will recommend it to their friends and report back to their advisors that the course was helpful. Student evaluations can serve as a monitor to student reactions.

There are classes on every college campus which succeed because they have a reputation for being easy. You do not want your course to fall within this group. A course can be popular because it is seen as highly beneficial and one in which students learn skills they can use. However, if the course is seen as being too difficult (or requiring too much work for one or 2 credit hours), then enrollment will suffer.

Textbooks may also be a factor in student enrollment. Many students have limited finances and may feel that they cannot afford to take an elective course, particularly for one or 2 credits, if the textbook is expensive.

Review again the checklist for effective teaching and make sure that you are doing all you can to meet student needs, teach clearly, grade fairly, and acquire student feedback. If the course is being taught effectively and it continues to meet student needs, then students will recommend it both to other students and to their advisors.

Dealing with Library Politics

Some library courses have been discontinued because of pressures from inside the library. In times of declining financial support, a course which reaches a relatively small number of students or which requires large amounts of staff time may be seen as less important to maintain than other library services. Do not wait until the threat arises. Make a consistent effort to keep the value of a course apparent and retain the support of others in the library.

Student evaluations can be used to demonstrate the course's worth. If you ask open-ended questions on course evaluations, you may find yourself with a bank of student quotes which are highly supportive of the class. Each time the course is taught, summarize the course evaluations (fairly, of course) by appending quotes, and submit a report to the director and others on the staff. If students appreciate your course—and most library courses seem to be appreciated—make sure it's known. If other kinds of evaluations are performed on the course, publicize these results as well.

Another key to library support is to involve other librarians. Ask for their input on the course and their reactions to assignments. Technical services librarians might be asked to give short presentations in class or the director might speak briefly on the future of libraries. Try to encourage the feeling that the course belongs to the library (which, in fact, it does).

Many courses have failed because they have been seen as belonging to one librarian, who receives recognition from students and faculty. Other librarians may resent the attention and be all too willing to attack the course. Rotating the teaching of the course again emphasizes that ownership of the course is retained by all the librarians.

Required courses are especially vulnerable to pressures from outside of the library. Both campus and departmental requirements change over time. Faculty or administrative supporters may leave, and others may not view the course as one which should be required. Student complaints to advisors or administrators will also erode campus support.

Using student and other evaluation results will allow you to monitor sources of student dissatisfaction, which you can then work to overcome. Providing copious examples of how students can use the course to their benefit will also increase their perception of the course's value. Again, results of evaluations should be shared with administrators and key faculty members. Articles in the school paper from time to time can also highlight the courses's achievements.

SUMMARY

Getting a library course off the ground requires the support of various groups. Library administrators and other members of the library staff must view it as something which benefits the entire library, not solely one librarian. Other campus support, particularly for required courses, must also be marshalled. Once the course is approved, students must be attracted to it.

Maintaining a library course means that *support* must be maintained. Both successes and failures of the course in meeting its objectives should be shared with those who make decisions as to the course's continuation. Much as the initiating librarian may want to view the course as his/her own creation, ownership must be shared with the library at large. Give credit to all the people you can.

FOR FURTHER READING

Morris, J.M. (1975). Gaining faculty acceptance and support of library instruction: A case study. In H. Rader (Ed.), *Faculty involvement in library instruction* (pp. 57–74). Fifth Annual Conference on Library Orientation for Adademic Libraries. Ann Arbor, MI: Pierian Press.
An account of one library's attempts to have a course approved by a curriculum committee.

Chapter 3:
Planning the Library Course

A successful library course does not just happen. It requires a great deal of planning. Much thought about the goals and objectives of the course and the model to be used must occur before any materials or lessons are developed. Unfortunately, this gestation period is often skipped over in the rush to actually get a course ready. We criticize our students for not thinking through what they need to know and for plunging into the process of gathering materials, yet we are also often guilty of the same shortsightedness.

Many people begin by asking themselves, "What should the course cover?" Answering this question often results in a hodge-podge of topics which have little or no relationship to each other, to an overall goal, or to what students need to know. A systematic approach in the design of a course will create a meaningful structure for the students. One system for course planning is to follow these steps:

1. Set an overall goal (or goals).
2. Analyze these goals to determine what they mean.
3. Derive objectives.
4. Select a model.
5. Develop assignments and tests from these objectives.
6. Write a syllabus.

SETTING AN OVERALL GOAL

The first step in any planning process is to think through what you actually want to accomplish. Goal statements are often dashed off in global terms which are nearly impossible to translate into actual classroom activities. This goal statement is typical of those produced when little thought has gone into them:

> Purpose of course: This course is designed to give students an appreciation of libraries and their organization and to develop lifelong strategies for solving information needs.

While this statement resonates with fine-sounding words, determining what it means in terms of what a course might be like is difficult. How do you teach students to appreciate libraries? What is meant by lifelong strategies? Moreover, how could you design a test which would measure student appreciation or use of lifelong strategies? And if these goals can't be measured, how would you know if the course was successful?

To begin thinking about goals, it is important to consider what the course is to accomplish. We talk about teaching library skills, which means that there are certain skills which we want students to have. We also want students to act differently: we want them to go about using a library in a different way after they've taken a library course. We are, in sum, talking about changing behavior, so a goal statement should be written in terms of the behaviors we want students to exhibit after instruction. When we know what the desired behaviors are, we will also know what we want to test for.

For some courses, it is easy to determine what is important for students to be able to do at the finish. In a legal research course, for example, students must be able to locate cases and write briefs. However, for a general course, goal setting may be more difficult. A common goal is that the course will create "effective library users" (a goal almost as global as "to create good citizens").

ANALYZING GOALS

What is meant by using a library effectively? What does someone who uses a library effectively do? Given 2 students, how can you tell which one is the effective library user? A good way to answer these questions is to brainstorm, alone or with others, the traits of an effective library user. If you have trouble getting started, think about what students do when they use a library ineffectively. One librarian came up with a list like this:

Ineffective library users:

- Look under only one subject heading.
- Plunge into gathering information before they know what they want.
- Use only the card catalog and the *Readers' Guide.*
- Are reluctant to ask for help.
- Are unaware of the existence of vast resources in periodical literature.
- Don't use (or even recognize) bibliographies and footnotes.
- Select materials that are outdated, irrelevant, or nonprofessional.
- Can't handle the mechanics of the tools.
- Skip the planning and thought stages.

The librarian could use the list to determine what traits should be developed.
Effective library users:

- Use many different subject headings.
- Gather information about their topics first and find out what they need to know.
- Use many different library tools.
- Ask for help when it's needed.
- Use periodical articles as well as books.
- Use bibliographies and footnotes to locate materials.
- Use materials at a level appropriate to their information needs.
- Know how to use basic tools and ask for help with unfamiliar advanced ones.
- Spend time at the beginning to plan out what they will do.

After looking at the list, the librarian realized that several traits were duplicates. By combining some traits and reworking the language on others, the refined list looks like this:
The effective library user:

- Can select and define a researchable topic by gathering background information, considering subtopics and alternative ways of looking at the topic, and determining if there is sufficient information.
- Can set up an efficient search strategy by selecting a researchable topic, generating search terms, determining what kind of tools will be most suitable, locating and using the tools, and then locating the materials.

● Can select materials at an appropriate level for the information need and can use the footnotes and bibliographies in these materials to locate further information.

By compiling a list of objectives, obtained from analyzing a goal (students will become effective library users) felt to be important, it's possible to see what it is that students would be able to do once they had achieved the goal. The objectives were specific enough that the librarian had an idea of the kinds of assignments to use and what to test for in order to see if students had indeed reached the goal.

Other librarians may or may not agree with this particular list of behaviors. However, it is the *process* which is important. There is no reason for setting goals if we do not know what they mean—if we cannot explain even to ourselves how we could tell if someone reached a goal.

The process of goal analysis also helps us focus on what is important and what is teachable. Take a fuzzy goal like "developing an appreciation of libraries." Analyzing this goal by asking, "What does someone do who appreciates libraries?" might result in a list like this:

● Uses many different libraries.
● Enjoys using libraries.
● Goes to a library when an information need arises.

These might all be things we'd like our students to do. But how do we teach someone to do them? And how do we tell if someone enjoys using a library? Do we want to base a course grade on how many times a student goes to a library? If we cannot teach a goal and cannot be reasonably certain that students reach the goal, then we ought not to be professing that this goal is one we wish to attain.

WRITING OBJECTIVES

Throughout this chapter, the emphasis has been on writing behavioral objectives. Not everyone agrees on the importance of objectives written in terms of student behavior. It is argued that they place an emphasis on only what is measurable and that this is sometimes trivial. It's true that we do want our students to understand, to appreciate, to enjoy. Writing behavioral objectives does not preclude these activities from happening, but it focuses our attention on those skills which we can demonstrate how to teach and on those skills which we can test for.

Objectives which are written in behavioral form are those which describe what students *do* —what we can see and, therefore, can measure. Nonbehavioral objectives often use terms like "know" or "appreciate." We cannot look into students' minds and tell when they "know" or "appreciate." We can, however, have students list, explain, or describe (which may connote knowing); behavioral objectives use verbs of behavior such as "list," "select," "compare," or "describe."

Writing behavioral objectives also helps us decide what is important to teach. Often what occurs in college classrooms is that the instructor gives out information, which students are expected to write down and be able to feed back to the instructor at the proper time. Thinking in terms of student behavior helps us devise ways of teaching that will encourage more than passive listening followed by regurgitation of information.

Teachers who have begun to use behavioral objectives find that they switch from thinking about content (and the first teaching method that comes to mind for teaching content is to give students the content) to thinking about how they want students to change. Changing behavior requires more than imparting content.

Almost 30 years ago, a hierarchical classification of behavioral objectives was developed and published. The classification, often referred to as Bloom's *Taxonomy* after Benjamin Bloom, the editor (Bloom, 1956), suggests this division:

1. Knowledge—students are able to recall facts and information.
2. Comprehension—students can interpret, translate, paraphrase information in their own way.
3. Application—students can apply knowledge in solving problems.
4. Analyzing—students can study a new situation and derive its major constituents.
5. Synthesizing—students can put constituents together in a new way.
6. Evaluating—students can set criteria and make judgements.

Under each category, the writers of Bloom's *Taxonomy* have listed dozens of objectives, written in behavioral terms, and multiple-choice test items which measure student attainment of the objectives.

Too often, we provide students with knowledge but expect that they will be able to understand, apply, analyze, and evaluate that information on their own. It's easier to write low-level objectives ("Students will be able to list...to define...") or no objectives at all. However, by identifying higher-level objectives (for example, "students will be able to evaluate the usefulness and appropriateness of a given bibliography), we can concentrate on teaching students to do what is really important.

"The card catalog" is a topic which appears often in course outlines. With no objective thought out, we may find ourselves talking about the history of card catalogs, their future manifestations, or detailed filing rules. What we probably really want, however, is for students to be able to use it: recognize its parts, manipulate its vagaries, and understand its limitations. Analyzing what is important to teach means that students can learn what is important to learn.

One day, a distraught author who was writing a book on careers in graphic arts approached a college librarian. In his hands he held 3 typewritten pages—a rough draft of a section on libraries. The information (gleaned from a brochure produced at a public library) covered Melvil Dewey, the parts of the Dewey Decimal system, looking up a subject in the card catalog, and, briefly, the *Readers' Guide.* A friend of his had told him that both Dewey and card catalogs were on the way out. What, he asked, should he do? Discard the already written section? He did think artists should know about libraries.

The librarian patiently talked to him about what artists might want to use a library for. For example, they might want books on artists or art history or on techniques and technological processes; they also might want to browse through current art journals. Graphic artists could use collections of typefaces, motifs, or borders, especially those that are uncopyrighted. Certainly they could use lists and directories of publications which buy art. And librarians could help in finding all these.

By this time, the author realized that it was not important, or even possible, to teach his readers in 3 pages how to use a library. He recognized that what he really wanted was to convince his audience that they should use libraries—and the best way to do this was to demonstrate how libraries would fit their needs. Once motivated, they'd find what they wanted. With a little bit of help, he set a goal, he analyzed it, and then he knew what he wanted to convey: that libraries have useful materials for artists. Here is a checklist for writing important objectives.

1. Set goals.
2. Analyze your goals: what must students be able to do to attain these goals?
3. Write these behaviors down.
4. Examine them for importance, redundancy, and relevancy.
5. Rewrite them in a form for students.

WRITING AN OUTLINE

After goals and objectives have been decided upon, you are then ready to write a course outline. The outline should, of course, flow from the objectives you have determined to be important. There are several different models of organization which have been commonly used in library courses. The one you select should be one which reinforces what you want to teach.

Tool Approach

This method of organization is the one most commonly found in textbooks on how to use a library. Assumed in the model is that there are certain library tools which students need to learn to use; the course therefore usually begins by examining the tool considered most important: the card catalog. An outline for this approach might be developed like this:

- Using the card catalog.
- Using different kinds of reference books.
- Using periodical indexes.
- Using other kinds of indexes.

This model would be appropriate if the major goal of the class was for students to be able to identify and use major tools. Its strength is that it is a traditional approach, one that both librarians and students feel comfortable with. Since students are likely to have had library instruction presented in this organization before, they can incorporate new information by adding to what they already know.

Its weakness is that tools are not an end in themselves. We use tools to do something. We do not learn to build a bookcase by being shown tools and having their use demonstrated; we learn to build a bookcase by building a bookcase and along the way, we can learn to use various tools as they're needed.

Librarians have frequently coped with this weakness by adding another part to the outline, one on researching papers. However, this may not be sufficient to tie it all together.

Search Strategy Approach

Many courses are set up according to a search strategy approach, which follows the same process often recommended for library research. An outline for this model would perhaps look like this:

- Choosing and limiting a topic.
- Locating and using background information.
- Locating and using bibliographies or research reviews.
- Locating and using monographic materials.
- Locating and using periodical materials.
- Locating and using other information (government documents, interviews, etc.)
- Using reference materials to locate specific facts.

This model is probably the best one for the course whose major objective is for students to learn a search strategy for writing papers. The organization itself reinforces what is being taught, since course materials are presented in the same order as the recommended search strategy. A weakness in this approach is that there may be objectives the instructor feels are important to cover, such as locating consumer information, but which do not fit easily into a search strategy process.

Discipline Approach

This type of organization is commonly used in library school reference courses and has sometimes been adapted to courses for undergraduate students. An outline for this approach might look like this:

- Introduction to basic tools (card catalog, etc.).
- Planning a research paper.

- Researching in the humanities.
- Researching in the social sciences.
- Researching in the sciences.

This approach emphasizes the commonality of sources in various fields. It also allows the logical use of guest lecturers ("tomorrow the art librarian will be here"). However, the model has serious drawbacks. A psychology student is seldom interested in, and will seldom use, the research tools of music or literature. Perhaps the model only fits the goal that students will understand the research process in various disciplines. What is gained in comprehensive coverage may well be lost by low student interest and motivation.

Types of Information Approach

A model that has been successfully used in adult education classes in public libraries is based upon the goal that class members will, rather than learning only one search strategy, be able to use different strategies to locate different types of information. Such an organization might look like this:

- Keeping up on current events.
- Finding out about people.
- Finding geographic and travel information.
- Finding facts and statistics.
- Finding consumer information.
- Finding "a good book to read."

College students, however, have different information needs from those of public library patrons. Student impetus for using a library almost always results from assignments. A similar model, based on student needs, might be outlined on this basis:

- Finding information for short papers and speeches.
- Researching the long paper.
- Evaluating materials.
- Locating quick facts and statistics.
- Researching a company or career.

This approach focuses on the use of alternative search strategies for different information needs and is thus more complex than one based on a single search strategy. Its strength is that it allows for more than just the extended, lengthy search and perhaps is more closely related to what students will need after college. Its weakness is that it does not create a sense of system in using the library.

Other Approaches

Classes for particular majors may have different outlines. Their organization may reflect a search strategy appropriate for or types of materials important to that discipline. Outlines may also be created around types of information problems that a professional might have to solve. The case study method described in Chapter 4, "Developing Materials for the Library Course," is an excellent example of a problem-solving method.

Developing an outline is not just a matter of selecting some topics that should be covered. The first step in creating a meaningful structure for students ought to be in devising an outline that is logical, makes sense to you and your students, and reinforces your objectives.

LAYING OUT THE COURSE

Once goals and objectives are set and an organization decided upon, it is time to get to the nitty-gritty of laying the course out and seeing how it will fit.

Begin by counting up the number of class sessions you will have. This may vary slightly from semester to semester. Assume that the first day will be largely taken up with housekeeping and getting-acquainted details, the last day perhaps with an exam. Compare this number with your outline. Approximately how many days do you want to devote to each topic?

After making a rough estimate, consider some other factors. Is there a day when you'll have an out-of-town meeting? If so, you might ask someone else to take the class for you, you might allow students that time to work on a major assignment, or you might want to schedule individual appointments in place of a class meeting.

Are there field trips which might be valuable to take? A tour behind the scenes in technical services might demonstrate the library system, or a trip to a related branch library might be helpful. While a trip or tour makes a nice change of pace, it should fit your course objectives.

Go back now to your rough estimate of days for each topic, and see if you want to change it. Figure out when tests or major assignments are due. You'll want to avoid scheduling them just after a holiday or vacation, when student absences, either physically or mentally, may be high. If it's possible without altering the structure, you may want to shift some topics around.

Some instructors like to assign a certain topic to each class meeting. Others prefer more flexibility. However, you should at least have a good idea of where you want to be each week, in order to avoid having to cover the last half of the course in the last week. With some sort of a schedule in mind, you are now ready to consider your syllabus.

WRITING A SYLLABUS

While the dictionary definition of a syllabus is that it is a list of goals or content for a course, a syllabus has come to mean more than that in higher education. It is often considered to be like a contract, one in which you inform students what the course is about and tell them what they are expected to do (in fact, in some court cases, the course syllabus has been regarded as a contract). Here are some of the items which should appear on a syllabus:

- Your availability: Name, office location, office hours, telephone number.
- Course name and number, number of credits (just in case anyone was confused).
- Course goals and objectives: The students should know what the course is intended to accomplish.
- Course content: Some instructors include only the course outline. Others indicate the dates when topics will be covered.
- Course requirements: What the students will be expected to do. Mention the number of tests and types of assignments. Give dates for major ones, so students can make note of them in their schedules.
- Basis for grading: For many students, this one will be the most important. While your actual measures may not be developed until later, you should know at this point how

you will be evaluating. The more information you can give students at this point, the less anxiety they will have.

● Textbook, if any: Give its citation, where available and price, whether it's required or recommended.

● Other readings, if any: List these, along with the dates they should be completed.

The syllabus plays a valuable part in setting the tone for a class. It conveys what you consider to be important and what you expect students to do. Including specific information on dates and assignments tells students that these are firm commitments and gives them the opportunity to plan ahead for them.

SUMMARY

The most important part (and often the hardest part) of planning a course is deciding what it is that you want students to be able to do when they finish it. Only by determining this will you be able to conceive an organization, content, assignments, and tests which are worthwhile and meaningful to students. Using the process of goal analysis to derive behavioral objectives helps you to focus on what is important, possible, and desirable.

REFERENCE

Bloom, Benjamin. (1956), *Taxonomy of educational objectives. Vol I: The cognitive domain.* Chicago: David McKay.

FOR FURTHER READING

Association of College and Research Libraries. Bibliographic Instruction Section. Policy and Planning Committee. (1979). *Bibliographic instruction handbook.* Chicago: American Library Association.
Includes a model statement of objectives, as well as a guide to writing objectives.

Mager, R.F. (1972). *Goal analysis.* Belmont, CA: Fearon Publishers.

Mager, R.F. (1973). *Measuring instructional intent: Or got a match?* Belmont, CA: Fearon Publishers.

Mager, R.F. (1975). *Preparing instructional objectives* (2nd ed.) Belmont, CA: Fearon Publishers.

The goal analysis model in this chapter is adapted from the book *Goal Analysis.* Anyone involved in teaching should read Mager; each book can be read in one short sitting and is highly entertaining as well as likely to change behavior.

Oberman, C, and Stauch, K. (1982). *Theories of bibliographic instruction: Designs for teaching.* New York: Bowker.

Several chapters give ideas for organizational approaches to bibliographic instruction.

Vargas, J.E. (1972). *Writing worthwhile behavioral objectives.* New York: Harper and Row.

A good introduction to the writing of objectives.

Chapter 4:
Developing Materials for the Library Course

This chapter is devoted to the practicalities of selecting and developing teaching materials, whether they be assignments, textbooks, handouts, or audiovisual materials. To be effective, these materials should be planned well in advance. Some teachers prefer to wait as long as possible; there's a certain adrenalin high which occurs while frantically standing in front of a photocopy machine moments before the class is to arrive. However, acceptable A-V materials cannot be put together the night before. In fact, many instructors recommend developing materials during slow periods such as summer or between semesters, which means planning well in advance. Finally, if materials are developed ahead of time, other library instructors can use them in similar classes.

DESIGNING ASSIGNMENTS

Assignments should follow course objectives and should require students to practice what you want them to be able to do when they complete the class. Developing assignments from objectives helps to focus on what is important for students to do and to ensure that the assignments make sense to the students. You want to avoid the students' feeling as though they're doing busy work which doesn't relate to a purpose. A common requirement is to have students look up a topic in an index and identify citations. If your objective is for students to demonstrate that they know how to use the tool, then having them locate one citation is sufficient.

Worksheets

While many college courses are taught in a lecture format, with perhaps exams and a paper, almost all library courses include assignments which ask students to apply the skills they're learning. Often these assignments take the form of completion of worksheets or workbooks, set up in a question-and-answer format. Worksheets can be of 2 types: (1) those that direct students to look for one specific answer ("look in the card catalog and find a book by Marvella Rival") or (2) those that ask students to find their own answers, based on their own topics ("use the *PAIS* to find an article on your subject").

DIRECTED EXERCISES

Exercises which ask students to look for specific answers are easy to grade. They can be multiple-choice or computer-scored. They allow the instructor to direct students' attention to what the instructor finds important. And, with this type of guidance, students should always be able to find an answer.

However, the time required to design the assignments may be more than the time gained in easier grading. Multiple sets of questions must be written to avoid students' simply copying one another's answers. Lacking motivation, students may not care about the answers, so their response may go from their eyes to their pencils, without ever passing through their minds. Finally, directed exercises can cause a great deal of wear-and-tear on library materials. After 500 students have looked at one page of the *Readers' Guide,* it will probably be defaced and in shreds and, at the very least, the correct response will be clearly marked. Librarians have coped with this problem by providing duplicate sets of materials (an expense to take into account) or by requiring the exercises to be completed in pencil. Multiple sets of questions which refer different students to different volumes and pages alleviate the problem as well, but these, of course, require much more development time.

GENERIC EXERCISES

Worksheets that ask students to look up their own topics in library tools seem far more satisfying to students and designing this type of assignment takes much less time than do directed exercises. Although grading generic exercises can take a great deal of time, after some practice, most librarians can look at student responses and have a sense of whether or not they are correct, checking only questionable answers in the original sources. However, some instructors may have a need to check every answer to make absolutely sure of accuracy. Those instructors who feel compelled to substantiate accuracy may not have enough time to use generic exercises.

Another problem with generic exercises is that not all topics will be appropriate for all tools. Indeed, some topics, such as very current ones, will not fit any. Some students will spend an exorbitant amount of time trying to find a topic in an unsuitable tool. In such cases, librarians should remind students that the point is to demonstrate use of the tool and that if their topic doesn't seem to fit, to use another one for that particular assignment. Each assignment should offer some flexibility in approach, depending on the student's topic. For example, humanities majors should be directed to choose a social concern of interest to them when looking for a topic in government documents.

In general, generic exercises are the best choice for classes up to 50 or so because of their greater degree of student involvement. However, for larger classes, specific-answer exercises may be necessary.

LAYOUT OF WORKSHEETS

Worksheets should be designed with wide margins, plenty of room in which to write and take notes, and with directions as concisely stated as possible. Directions which try to anticipate every possible situation are confusing and encourage students to ignore them. A good device is to ask for feedback on the worksheet. Ask students to mention when directions are confusing and to make suggestions for improvement. Keep track of questions consistently answered incorrectly. Listen to the questions students ask about assignments.

APPROPRIATE USE OF WORKSHEETS

Worksheets which ask students to use library tools to locate bits of information or citations are appropriate when the objective is simply to teach students to use certain library tools. However, worksheets like these cannot teach students higher-level objectives, such as selecting appropriate materials, viewing the library as a system, or being able to devise the best strategy to satisfy an information need.

Can worksheets address higher-level objectives? Easily, if the worksheets ask for written responses. For example, a periodicals worksheet could ask students to locate citations from a general index, a specialized index, and an abstracting service; to use the citations to locate articles from a general magazine and a professional journal; and to compare the articles in terms of the authors' credentials, use of evidence, and bibliography.

The instructor's task becomes more difficult if the answers must be multiple-choice; however, it's still possible to address these objectives with them. For example, a worksheet might direct a student to 2 specific articles and have questions which point out the differences between them. For example:

- Which author is probably a journalist?
- Which article refers you to other sources?
- Which article is from a periodical which receives much of its revenue from advertising?
- Which article is best for getting a quick idea of the topic?
- Which article is best for serving as a source of information for an upper-level paper?

Diaries and Journals

Another commonly used assignment in library courses is to have the student keep a diary or journal describing what the student did in the process of completing an extended search. If the object of keeping a journal is to see if the student can describe a good search strategy, then it is probably valuable. If the object is to determine what the student actually *did,* then the assignment probably fails. If students know they are to be graded on the journal, they may respond with what they feel will give them the best grade—not always an honest response. Keeping a diary can be an unpopular assignment, since diaries require a great deal of time, and students rarely sense their value. The ability to keep a diary or journal is probably not an objective of a library course. Other types of assignments, which have students practice what you want them to learn, will probably meet objectives better and result in greater student motivation. If the primary purpose of the journal is to determine if the student can describe a good search strategy, then a better way of ascertaining it is to ask this as an examination question.

A variation of a diary, usually called a "research log," may be more effective. Typically, a research log consists of the rough jottings of notes: lists of possible search terms, library tools used, suggestions of topic definitions. A research log resembles the kind of notes a researcher should be keeping and, thus, may help students formulate good note-taking techniques. Asking that the research log be turned into a neat, typewritten summary may require more time than it warrants. Some librarians have students hand in only their rough copy as the course progresses, as a check on whether they are keeping up. If you outline a structured format, students have guidance in learning the type of information to include.

Search Projects

Library courses often have as a culminating assignment the completion of a bibliography. This may range from a simple bibliography of 10 to 20 items on a topic to an annotated bibliography designed to be as complete as indicated in a statement of scope. If a major objective of the course is to teach a search strategy or to be able to identify core literature, then this can be a very successful assignment. Students' motivation will be higher if they are allowed to choose their own topics and highest if the topic is one they can use for a research paper or project in another class.

If one of the course objectives is for students to be able to select and define a researchable topic, then a logical assignment is to have students practice this skill by requiring them to write a topic statement or scope note which succinctly defines the topic and indicates the parameters used. Following is an example:

> Directions for Writing a Scope Note. The purposes of writing a scope note are to define the topic and state the primary objective of the bibliography, to explain the organization of the bibliography, and to note the parameters of the search (e.g., time, level, audience, and other methods of selecting what is included). To write a scope note, answer the following questions about your bibliography:
>
> 1. What is the title? What does the title mean?
> 2. What are the objectives of the bibliography? To be comprehensive? To be selective? If selective, what are the criteria to be used?
> 3. For whom has the bibliography been developed? Scholars?

Students? General public?
4. What languages are represented in the bibliography? Are the sources national or international?
5. What types of material does the bibliography include? Books? Journal articles? Primary sources?
6. How is the bibliography to be arranged? Alphabetically? Chronologically? By subject? By type of material?
7. What time period is covered?

Your scope note should probably be about a paragraph, written in standard English. Your reader should have a good idea of what to expect in your bibliography.

Sample Scope Note: Behavior Modification Techniques in the Classroom. "Behavior modification" is a term used to describe attempts to change behavior by using reinforcement techniques—that is, by rewarding immediately behavior that is desired. These techniques have been used extensively in education over the last 15 years, primarily to control disruptive behavior. This bibliography lists pertinent published accounts of research occurring in actual classrooms in the United States over the last 15 years. Excluded are general articles designed to introduce laypersons or teachers to the idea of behavior modification, textbooks, and other secondary sources. Entries are arranged chronologically.

If an objective of the course is that students should locate and use all appropriate library tools, then you will probably also want to ask students to turn in a list of the tools they used. You should also ask them to rate the ones they found most useful and tell why.

Still another objective which can be met by this assignment is that students will be able to evaluate the materials they've found. If this is your objective, then you may want students to indicate primary sources, or level of sophistication, or most useful ones.

This assignment has the danger of overwhelming the students. Librarians may be able to do such a task quickly, but, for students, it will be a new experience and may take them far longer than you (and they) had supposed. If the assignment is to be handed in at the end of the course, make sure that students do not put off working on it. Require parts of it to be handed in as the course progresses, so that everyone has made a start on it.

Problem-Oriented Assignments

This kind of assignment works extremely well with courses which are planned for certain majors. Assignments are designed which relate to the kinds of problems these majors will have to solve, either in college or as professionals. Business majors, for example, can be given a marketing problem which may require them to use reference books, statistical tools, and business periodicals. Education majors could be asked to take a certain teaching method and examine the research related to it.

Problem-oriented assignments can also be used for general courses. For example, researching careers or job opportunities is interesting to almost all students. To meet an objective that students use different kinds of strategies for various information needs, assignments can be organized around these strategies. For example, students can be told that they have been asked to give a 10-minute speech on a topic of current interest and that they are to identify useful library tools and locate sufficient materials at an appropriate level.

Still another form of problem solving is to create a complex case study which requires the use of a number of different approaches and library tools to solve. Students may work on these individually or in groups. Cerise Oberman and Rebecca Linton (1982) describe an elaborate case study, in which students working in a group are told that, as interns to a state senator, they are to prepare a background report on the issue of nuclear waste transportation. In a series of directions, they are asked to identify the scope of the problem by making a list of the questions they need to answer; to analyze the scope of the problem by determining what issues to address; to generate possible solutions by listing possible sources and identifying them as primary or secondary sources; to devise a search strategy; and, finally, to gather the needed information.

Case studies like these are intrinsically interesting to students (this approach is used extensively in law and other professional schools). Students can become deeply involved with them and care about solving the problem. Designing such a case study requires creativity and imagination and is not an easy task; however, the results can certainly justify the efforts, since the results are usually highly motivated students.

Other Assignments

Depending upon your objectives, many other kinds of effective assignments can be developed. One librarian has as a course objective that students will be able to use other libraries. The best way for students to learn to use other libraries is to use them. She developed a list of questions about locations, services, collections, etc., and told her students to visit another large library. In order to answer the questions, they had to walk around the library, observe, and ask for information. Students were asked for comments at the end, and they responded by saying things as, "Now I know I can find my way around an unfamiliar library," or "The librarians were so helpful!" They learned that they could walk into another library, find their way around, and safely ask questions. Some guidelines for developing good assignments are as follows:

- Assignments should flow from the goals and objectives of the course. They should require the students to do those things you want them to be able to do. If course objectives other than being able to use specific library tools are included, then assignments should not be restricted to fill-in-the-blank worksheets.
- The purpose of the assignment should be clear. Students should know why they are doing the assignments. If they don't recognize the point, then what *is* the point?
- Directions should be clearly and briefly stated. The longer they are, the less likely they are to be read.
- The first time a new assignment is used, it should be considered a trial run. Students will respond in unexpected ways; directions that seemed perfectly clear will prove obtuse.
- Feedback should be solicited from students. They will tell you whether the assignment was confusing, seemed worthwhile, or was pointless. Asking how much time the assignment took to complete will also help to get an idea of whether it was well-planned. Listen to the responses.
- Problems should be noted, perhaps on a blank copy of the assignment. Otherwise, you'll forget those minor points which caused everyone problems when it is time to revise assignments for the next semester.

READING MATERIALS

Some library courses have no outside reading for students and instead, rely upon the class lectures and assignment directions to impart information. However, the use of a text, reserve readings, or handouts can present students with alternative points of view, serve as a springboard for discussion, and reinforce concepts covered in class.

Textbooks

Many library courses do not require textbooks; some use locally produced texts. Few of the courses described in the case studies in this book use commercially prepared texts. Why? The usual answer is that "no text seemed appropriate for the course." In addition, many library courses concentrate on the specific services and tools of that particular library.

An annotated list of some currently available commercial texts appears in the "Other Resources" section of this book. Most of them use a "tool" approach, with perhaps a chapter on writing a paper. If you choose one of these and your objectives cover more than how to use tools, you will probably have to supplement the text with reserve readings or additional exercises.

Locally produced textbooks are certainly an option for librarians to consider, particularly in independent study courses where directions for the course are part of the text. They may be typed and reproduced in the library, or, if there are sufficient funds, printed; they may be sold in the college bookstore in order to recoup some of the costs.

Like any printed materials that you want people to actually read, locally produced textbooks should be well-laid out with double spacing and wide margins on all 4 sides. Headings should be used generously in order to break up long pages of text and to help students understand the organization.

Reserve Readings

Carefully chosen readings can often supplement a textbook or substitute for one. These readings might range from portions of library textbooks to scholarly discussions of the nature of information structure. In courses where students are majoring in many different subjects, the librarian can select readings describing research in, say, humanities, social sciences, and the sciences, and direct students to read only those which are appropriate for their interests or majors.

HANDOUTS

Probably every college class uses handouts, and they can be an effective teaching tool; in some cases, they can substitute for a text. Handouts in an outline form, with space for students to write, serve to reinforce the organization of a lecture; providing directions for assignments on the outline helps students use their time efficiently.

Always discuss any handouts you distribute. Avoid passing out reams of paper which are never talked about, since this gives students the idea that what is occurring in class is of no importance.

Again, if you want students to read what you give them, pay attention to the layout. Have wide margins, double space if there are more than 4 or 5 lines, avoid faded dittos, and keep information concise and to the point.

AUDIOVISUAL MATERIALS

Transparencies, slides, tapes, and videocassettes are all commonly used in library courses. Like any teaching tool, they need to be carefully planned for and developed. Of this group, only transparencies can be produced on short notice (and then only if you have ready access to the right supplies and equipment). The others require considerable lead time; therefore, the decision to use audiovisual materials must be made sometime before the course begins.

Many commercial audiovisual materials exist for library instruction in elementary and secondary schools. However, with the exception of Oak Woods Media (listed in the "Other Resources" section of this book), commercial materials produced for college library instruction tend to be both technically and instructionally poor. For the time being, at least, librarians will have to rely primarily on their own local resources.

Transparencies

The overhead projector is one of the most commonly used teaching tools. Its major advantages are that it allows the teacher to control what the student is looking at, face the audience and maintain eye contact while using it, and be able to keep lights at least partially on. Transparencies can be produced on almost any recently manufactured copier at a relatively low cost. Transparencies can be made of pages from library tools, so that the use of a tool can be easily demonstrated. They can be written on with a marker, thus replacing a chalkboard, and color can be added to them. Students can better understand the organization of a lecture if an outline of the major points is presented on a transparency. Any line drawing can be easily reproduced; pertinent cartoons can help to make a point.

However, the overhead is also one of the most misused teaching tools. The major fault is attempting to use transparencies which do not project large enough for students to read. Typewritten lines on a transparency cannot be read past the first few rows in a classroom; the same can be said for most printed pages.

Many libraries or copy centers have copiers which enlarge. It will usually take 2 or 3 enlargements for a normal typewritten or printed page to be legible on a transparency. The whole page will not fit; if you want students to be viewing a whole page while you talk, you should distribute photocopies of it.

If you do not have access to an enlarging copier, you can use the Orator element on a Selectric typewriter to produce larger letters. However, hand printing a list of points (which is large enough to be readily seen) is far preferable to a neater, but smaller, typewritten list.

Good transparencies can also be made by creating an original on a personal computer with good graphic capabilities. The Apple Macintosh, for example, can produce large lettering as well as graphs, borders, and patterns which will reproduce well on a transparency.

If there is a printing office on campus, this office will likely have a 3-M Platemaker or its equivalent, which can be used to enlarge transparencies. Since this is a more expensive process, you would probably only want to use it to enlarge index entries and other samples which would be used frequently.

In addition to using colored markers on transparencies, color can be added through applying color adhesive film. This film and other accessories are available at local business stores or through a 3-M supplier.

Any black or red line drawing reproduces well onto a transparency. A one-time purchase of a clip-art book (the American Library Association sells one and any art supply catalog will list many others) can provide borders, cartoons, and other illustrations. If you look around, you will notice many drawings from advertisements, books, and magazines, which you can clip or copy and save for future use. Black-and-white cartoons reproduce well, and the use of a cartoon makes a good change of pace in the classroom. Even black-and-white photographs will occasionally reproduce well, if you are not interested in fine detail. Some tips on using overhead transparencies:

- Use the "revelation" technique. This means simply to place a piece of paper on top of the transparency and reveal in sequence the topics discussed. This prevents students from skipping ahead of the presentation and encourages better attention.
- Use colored markers to highlight. This is especially helpful in situations such as showing an entry from an index. A red circle around the volume number helps the student locate the number. Be sure to use water-soluble markers if the transparency is to be used again.
- Look at the transparency on the projector rather than pointing to the projected image or turning around to read the information from the screen. A major advantage of the overhead is that you can maintain eye contact with the audience. Do so.
- Ensure that lights can be left on by having transparencies large enough and by projecting onto a screen rather than a wall.
- Make your transparencies large enough to be seen; keep them simple.

Slides

Slides are also an easy medium to produce. Using a series of slides is often an effective way to "tour" the library so that everyone can see and hear. Slides may be used to illustrate a search strategy or to show a tool to the whole class. The ability to show photographs of people, use color, and to control audience attention makes slides a more powerful teaching tool than transparencies.

Almost everyone has access to a 35mm camera. However, if you have access on your campus to a professional photographer, take advantage of it. Most libraries are lit fluorescently, a tricky lighting situation under which to make good photographs. In addition, the photographer will have a copy stand, which makes taking photographs of book pages much easier than hand-holding a camera.

Before investing in the time and expense of taking slides, decide what you want your series of slides to do. What are your objectives? From your objectives, determine the organization and content. Write down just what each slide should cover. If you are illustrating the use of a library tool, write down the steps involved in its use—even such small ones as consulting the periodical holdings list—to make sure you haven't left one out.

Never present more than one point per slide. Usually, you will want several slides to illustrate each point. A common method is to use a long shot to orient the audience to an area, then use closer shots so that they can see detail. The audience needs to be able to place what it's seeing in perspective and to understand what it's seeing.

On a piece of paper, write down on half of it what the content is to be; on the other half, what the slide is to depict. For example, here is what a listing might look like for a series which has as its objectives that students will be able to find the *Readers' Guide,* use it to locate a citation, interpret the citation, and locate the article it refers to.

Content:

1–3. Locating *Readers' Guide.*

4. Choosing a bound recent issue.
5–6. Locating an entry.

7–17. Interpreting an entry: abbreviations, titles, volume numbers, page numbers, dates.

Slide:

1. Long shot of index area.
2. Medium shot of index table.
3. Close-up of volumes.
4. Close-up of bound volume and paper issue.
5. Shot of entire page.
6. Close-up of one entry.*
7. Close-up, with author underlined in red.*
8. Title underlined in red.*
9. Abbreviation underlined in red.*

Content: Slide:

                                 10. Entire abbreviation page.*
                                 11. Close-up of particular
                                     abbreviation.*
                                 12. Periodical title underlined
                                     in red.*
                                 13. Heading on periodical
                                     abbreviation page.*
                                 14. Close-up of particular
                                     abbreviation.*
                                 15. Volume number under-
                                     lined in red.*
                                 16. Page numbers underlined
                                     in red.*
                                 17. Date underlined in red.*
18–19. Determining if the   18. Periodical list lying on
library has the periodical.   table.
                                 19. Close-up of particular
                                     entry.*
20–24. Locating periodical.   20. Student going upstairs.
                                 21. Student looking at peri-
                                     odical stacks.
                                 22. Student looking at shelf
                                     guides.
                                 23. Shelf of periodicals, with
                                     particular volume pulled
                                     out.
                                 24. Close-up of actual article.*

The asterisk denotes a copy stand shot. The index pages can be shot from multiple photocopies of the page or a small, colored pointer can be moved for each shot.

Are all of these slides necessary? The answer is certainly yes, if these are the actual steps involved in using an index to locate a periodical article. Illustrating the steps like this makes it clear to the student exactly what is to be done in a way that words cannot. Writing down what each slide is to show guarantees that you will not forget one; giving a photographer such a list ensures gratitude, since the instructions have been clearly thought out and communicated. To use slides effectively, remember these tips:

● Avoid lingering on each slide. Thirty seconds is probably sufficient. Several different shots taken from various angles, and shown for 5 or 10 seconds each, are far better than one slide left on too long.

- Keep the presentation brief and snappy. Fifteen minutes is probably an adequate amount of time to devote to slides.
- Make one point per slide and stick to that point. Don't show one thing and talk about another.
- Always run through your slides quickly before class. Even though you think there's no way they could get out of order or be in upside down, it happens. You only want comic relief when you've planned it.

Slide-Tapes

Slide-tapes are not just slides accompanied by sound. They are packaged productions, and thus audiences expect more from them. Consider the possibilities of adding music, special sound effects, and different voices.

Slide-tapes are often prepared with a single-voice narration, with perhaps a little music at the beginning and end. In a classroom presentation, you are better off by merely showing the slides and delivering a live and, therefore, more engaging narration. You will have saved time and money, the equipment will be easier to set up and use, and student reaction will probably be better. However, well-done slide-tapes, using the special effects possible with them, do an excellent job of attracting and maintaining student attention. Professional presentations are almost as effective as video or film, while being far less expensive and easier to update.

As with any teaching materials, slide-tapes should be carefully planned. Determine first what you want the slide-tape to accomplish. What should students be able to do after viewing it? After setting objectives, select a model. Slide-tapes lend themselves well to telling a story, which is an effective way of holding attention.

Writing the script comes next. A simple way of doing this is to have a sheet of paper or card for each slide. Write the narration (keeping it brief) on half of the paper, and use the other half, as for the slides-only presentation, to describe what the slide should depict. Produce the slides, then go through them carefully to make sure that the narration fits the slide. Have others view them as well and incorporate their suggestions into the presentation. The tape should then be recorded in a soundproof room. Add music, sound effects, use other voices. If you have access to professional editing through your local campus learning resources center, take advantage of it.

Slide-tapes can be an effective teaching tool, lending color and interest to a classroom. However, they must be planned well in order to be effective: estimates of time involved to produce a slide-tape range up to 100 hours. If you cannot take the time to plan and execute a slide-tape well, you are better off not doing it at all.

Videotapes

Videotapes are being used increasingly in library instruction. Many campuses have the equipment to produce them; many libraries have the equipment to play them back. However, unless you have access to professional advice and technicians, do not attempt to produce a videotape yourself. Today's students have been raised on a steady diet of commercial television with extensive special effects, and they will not respond well to a jumpy, amateurish effort.

Videotapes carry the immediacy of film and are an excellent means of telling a story, involving students, and holding attention. All of these characteristics should be exploited. Simply videotaping a lecture results in a boring presentation. This technique, called B.T.H. (Big Talking Head), almost killed educational use of television in its early days.

However, if you have access to a production unit on campus and sufficient resources (a conservative estimate for a 10- to 15-minute videotape is $10,000), then videotapes may be a good option for you. After goals and objectives have been set, rely on your campus experts to help you script it and to execute the production.

A note here on content: many locally produced videotapes and slide-tapes are based on a common story line. A student, upset either because a library assignment was forgotten or that it was made at all, goes unwillingly off to the library. There, s/he meets a smug, all-knowing librarian who pedantically reveals the mysteries of the library. Who wants to identify with the stupid student as depicted? Nobody. Moreover, this story line implies that using a library is something that students inherently dislike and put off. If bibliographic instruction librarians don't convey the idea that library research can be interesting and rewarding, even exciting, then who will?

There are some notable exceptions. *Battle of the Superstars* (Library, Ohio State University) pits 2 students against each other in a race to see who can use the online catalog and periodical indexes the fastest and best. Commercials for other library services are interspersed. Some librarians find the humor overdone, but student response has been positive.

An excellent series of videotapes has been produced for a required freshman-level course at Western Kentucky University. *Library Trek,* (Helms-Craven Library, Western Kentucky University) for example, shows Captain Kirk and Mr. Spock being beamed down to a deserted library. Using Mr. Spock's considerable powers, they figure out the use and layout of the library and investigate a COM catalog. Another videotape in the series features a wonderland Alice finding her way through periodicals with frustrating hints given to her by a Cheshire cat.

At both of these institutions, the videotapes were produced by local campus units staffed by proficient technicians and writers. Professional actors or theater students were used. The productions were expensive. In one case, a grant was obtained; in the other, a vice president was very supportive. In both cases, the results were extremely effective.

Other Types of Media

Library courses seldom use films, filmstrips, or opaque projectors, and there is good reason for this. Films require a financial investment similar to videotapes, and they are more difficult to update. Filmstrip production requires equipment unlikely to be found locally and filmstrips' major advantages—compact storage and inexpensive duplication—are not necessarily helpful to classroom teachers. Opaque projectors were used much more commonly before the advent of easily made transparencies. While an opaque projector allows an instructor to show actual objects to an entire class, the equipment is bulky, loud, and cumbersome to use. Moreover, it produces enough heat to damage some types of materials. Most teachers opt for the convenience of an overhead or slides.

DEVELOPING MODULES FOR INDEPENDENT STUDY

Videocassettes and slide-tapes can be used effectively to set up individual learning stations. They may be made available for students to view when class presentations are missed, or they may be part of a learning package.

Preparing materials for independent study should follow the same process as that used for any materials production: set goals and objectives, select a medium, choose a model, write a script, produce it, and keep track of revisions to be made. When producing the material, however, do not view the student as only a passive receiver. Learning will be greater if the student is asked to provide answers and to manipulate materials.

For example, interaction can be provided by asking students to fill out a worksheet during the course of the presentation. Even better is to have actual materials as part of the learning package— a card catalog drawer, a book, an index volume. The student can then be told, for example, to look up a topic in the index and write down the pertinent information. Arrange for this in a slide-tape by having the student stop the presentation. On a videotape, time will have to be built in.

Computer-Assisted Instruction

Computers can, of course, be highly interactive. With a computer program, the computer can ask the question, and students can type in the answer and receive immediate feedback as to whether the answers are right or wrong. Computer-assisted instruction (CAI) is beginning to be used extensively in library instruction at the postsecondary level. The University of Delaware, for example, has produced a package of 5 lessons plus a test for their instruction program. Freshmen students first take a self-guided tour, and then use any PLATO terminal on campus to complete the lessons.

Putting materials on a computer may be an administrator's first response to dealing with large numbers of students. However, this response is viable only if the institution is willing to commit the necessary resources. Patricia Arnott, bibliographic instruction coordinator at the University of Delaware, estimates that their program required 700 hours in development and planning, and 2,000 to 3,000 hours in programing, review, and testing.

CAI requires librarians who are trained in writing programed instruction. On a few campuses, librarians who have learned programing also write the software; otherwise, close work with programers is necessary.

At the present time, software is available commercially for elementary and secondary library instruction. College-level software should be available soon. The University of Delaware, for example, plans to market its CAI within the near future. Colleges without the resources to develop their own software should find that CAI programs can be purchased. When this is possible, computers will probably be the medium of choice for independent study.

REFERENCES

Copies of *Battle of the Superstars* are available on loan from Project LOEX, Eastern Michigan University, Ypsilanti, MI 48197.

For more information on obtaining copies of *Library Trek,* contact Nancy Russell, Bibliographic Instruction Librarian, Helms-Craven Library, Western Kentucky University, College Heights, KY 42101. Other titles are also available as part of a series.

Oberman, C., and Linton, R. A. (1982). Guided design: teaching library research as problem-solving. In C. Oberman and K. Stauch (Eds.), *Theories of bibliographic instruction* (pp. 117–133). New York: Bowker.

FOR FURTHER READING

Gore, D. (1969). Teaching bibliography to college freshmen. *Educational Forum, 34,* 111–125.
Contains descriptions of interesting assignments for a library class.

Hardesty, L. (1978). *Use of slide/tape presentations in academic libraries.* New York: J. Norton.
Contains a survey of presentations, as well as a section on production and a bibliography.

Kemp, J.E. (1980). *Planning and producing audiovisual materials.* (4th ed.). New York: Harper and Row.
One of the most useful compendiums of information on how to design and create slides, tapes, transparencies, and videotapes.

Knapp, P. (1966). *The Montieth College library experiment.* Metuchen, NJ: Scarecrow Press.

A number of imaginative and effective assignments are described throughout the book, which is perhaps still the most valuable single work on bibliographic instruction.

Project Loex, Eastern Michigan University, Ypsilanti, MI 48197.

LOEX (Library Orientation Exchange) maintains a clearinghouse for bibliographic instruction materials. Members of LOEX may borrow samples of exercises, guides, audiovisual materials, etc. *Loex Newsletter,* sent to all members, carries announcements of new materials as well as other information of interest to instruction librarians.

3M Company.

3M is the largest producer of overhead transparency materials. Your local dealer will provide, with only a soft sell, a workshop on effective use of an overhead projector.

Chapter 5:
Teaching the Library Course

Regardless of how much time and effort has gone into planning, it is the day-to-day occurrences in a classroom that will influence the attitudes and learning of the students and give the teacher a sense of success or failure. Classroom effectiveness is a crucial part of the course. This chapter is intended to summarize what is known about effective teaching and to give suggestions for improving classroom instruction.

WHAT IS EFFECTIVE TEACHING?

Most people feel that, like art, they can recognize a good teacher when they see one—although they may be as hard-pressed to describe the qualities of an effective teacher as they are to define the qualities of a good painting.

Historically, ideas of what constitutes good teaching have been developed from this process: groups of people (who might be students, other teachers, or supervisors) have been asked to describe good (or bad) teachers. These responses have then been compiled into lists of characteristics, which can be used as a rating scale. This process is the basis for student rating scales, which are the most common form of evaluating teaching in higher education. There are a number of scales in use. Some have been commercially prepared, while others have been developed by individual institutions and departments. Most of these scales have many items in common. Wotruba and Wright (1975) examined 21 studies which developed scales and listed their characteristics. The following characteristics appeared in at least a third of the studies:

- Communication skills—interprets abstract ideas and theories clearly.

- Attitudes toward students which are favorable.
- Knowledge of the subject.
- Good organization of the subject matter and course.
- Enthusiastic about the subject.
- Fair in examinations and grading.
- Willing to experiment—flexible.
- Encourages students to think for themselves.
- Pleasant personality or personal appearance.
- Interesting as lecturer—good speaking ability.
- Instructor as a "worthwhile human being."

After years of the exposure to student rating scales, it is safe to say that it is clear what students like in teachers. However, it is *not* clear whether or not students learn more from teachers they like.

One series of interesting studies (often called the Doctor Fox experiments) involved the hiring of a professional actor to deliver a lecture to a class of students. He was witty, charming, entertaining—but his planned lecture was contradictory and non-substantive. The students rated him highly as an instructor (Ramagli and Greenwood, 1980). Some people in higher education have used these studies to argue that presentation skills are indeed very important; others have used them to argue that student rating scales measure only the entertainment value of an instructor.

There have been a few studies which have indicated some correlations between student ratings and student learning (for a summary of the research, see Centra, 1981, pp. 36–38). However, it seems that there is probably more involved in effective teaching than just those characteristics usually listed on a student rating scale.

In attempting to define what constitutes an effective teacher, researchers at the elementary and secondary level have developed other approaches besides asking people what they think a good teacher is or does. In the past 10 years, researchers have compared what happens in a classroom with subsequent scores on standardized tests and used advanced statistical techniques to analyze large numbers of studies at once. This method, called "product-process" research, has yielded some interesting results. For example, while there are no "generic" teaching skills, that is, specific behaviors that are best in all situations, teachers do make a difference; certain teachers do produce higher levels of student learning than others. These teachers tend to be those who take their role as teachers seriously and whose classes are organized to make good use of time. "Direct instruction"—teacher-controlled classes and much low-level questioning—appears to work best for students to master basic skills (Brophy, 1979).

Most of the process-product research has been conducted in primary grade classrooms and has been concerned with student mastery of the skills which are tested through standardized tests. While the research cannot at this point be generalized to higher education settings, it is apparent that the classroom dynamics have a great deal of effect on the learning which occurs.

What, then, can a librarian interested in being an effective teacher do? By synthesizing the research, debate, and thought that has occurred over the past 20 years, it is possible to identify a number of different factors that are important in increasing classroom learning.

TEACHER CHARACTERISTICS

Items that refer to teacher characteristics are the ones that appear most often on student rating scales. Personal characteristics of a teacher are important but not the only factors in creating a good learning environment.

Knowledge

The knowledge that you bring to the classroom is important. You must know something about the subject in order to teach it. Even if you prefer to be viewed as a facilitator, and not a fount of information, you must at least know enough to get the students started on the road to learning.

Presentation Skills

Students like good presentation skills. If much information is to be imparted by lecturing, then obviously the lecturer should be able to lecture well.

Not everyone has good presentation skills. Those who do not are usually aware that they do not. In fact, in a list of the "14 worst human fears," speaking before a group ranked number 1—while death was number 6 (Wallechinsky, 1977, p. 469). Those whose presentations are weak and who are uninterested in improving them should consider other forms of teaching—discussion, design of independent study, or the use of media—instead of lecturing.

Those interested in improving presentation skills can do so. The first step is to find out what skills are weak. Lists of good presentation skills usually mention these:

- *Eye contact.* Look at the people in the audience. If this is frightening, look just over the heads of the audience.
- *A natural delivery.* Speak from notes rather than reading from a prepared script. Some good lecturers write their main points ahead of time on a chalkboard or overhead transparency, and this suffices for their notes. The omission of several small points will not be noticed by an audience; being tied to a piece of paper will be.
- *Good body language.* Many college instructors are attached to their lecterns. Doing away with a lectern will probably result in more natural and relaxed body movement (and also lessen dependence on notes).
- *Good vocal delivery.* You should of course be heard. Vocal variety also adds interest to your presentation, so speak louder or slower for emphasis or suddenly drop your voice to a whisper (a technique guaranteed to gain the attention of everyone in the room). Lack of vocal variety results in a monotone.
- *Avoidance of repetitive, annoying personal mannerisms.* Speakers often adopt a gesture (stroking a beard or clicking a pen) or vocal tic ("you know," "if you please"). Repeating these mannerisms over and over again is at first merely annoying to listeners, and then maddening.

The skills listed above are not the only factors involved in a good presentation. A good presentation also involves the content, the student interaction, and the class environment. However, those points listed are the major mechanical skills involved in speaking before a group. Bad speaking habits, like any habits, are difficult to change. Asking another librarian to sit in on a class and identify problem behaviors from a checklist lets you know which skills need to be changed.

Once weak skills are identified, you should work on strengthening them one at a time. A reminder, such as a sign at the back of the room or a rubber band on the wrist, is a big help for eliminating a bad speaking habit. One good teacher, told in a student evaluation that he had an annoying habit of jingling coins in his pocket, asked his next semester's classes to tell him when he did it. They thoroughly enjoyed doing so (and perhaps paid closer attention to him) and his habit soon disappeared.

Ability to Communicate Abstractions

Another important teacher characteristic is the ability to communicate abstractions. Since we understand (or should understand) the concepts that are to be presented, we sometimes do not comprehend the difficulty that students have in understanding those concepts which are completely new to them.

The effective teacher uses many analogies and models, for example, comparing a divided catalog to the white and yellow pages of a telephone book. A librarian at Mankato State explains the use of the Boolean "and" by saying that a person who asks at an ice cream parlor for a chocolate and vanilla cone gets one scoop of each. A person who asks a computer for "chocolate and vanilla" gets 2 scoops of chocolate and vanilla swirled together.

An excellent way to practice making abstractions clear is to explain them to a nonlibrarian. Spouses or other long-suffering friends will be frank when they don't understand, and the process of explanation will often trigger useful analogies and metaphors.

The use of jargon also increases the level of abstraction. Like any discipline, librarians have developed a language in which brief terms are used to represent complex concepts. We speak of "manual access," when we mean that one uses a book or other printed tool to find materials; or "citation" when what we mean is the complete information needed to locate an item; or "monograph" when we mean a book complete unto itself, but more substantial than a pamphlet. Some of these terms mean different things to many nonlibrarians: for example, a "monograph" to a historian means a definitive work on a discrete subject.

Here are some terms, used widely in libraries, which librarians at one institution have found that their students do not understand:

- Citation.
- Circulate.
- Monograph.
- Bibliography versus biography (they are familiar with these 2 terms, but invariably get them confused).

- Annotated bibliography.
- Access.
- Abstract.
- Journal.
- Professional literature.
- Primary source or secondary source.
- Database searching.
- Vertical file.
- Discipline.

Use of such terms without a full explanation of what they stand for guarantees student confusion. Moreover, most undergraduate students are not secure enough in their own knowledge to tell the instructor when they do not understand terms and concepts.

Teacher Attitude

The teaching style of the instructor is not important. Good teachers can be authoritarian or democratic; information givers or group facilitators. However, a common characteristic of good teachers, as indicated in product-process research, is that they believe that what they're doing is important. The teacher who considers his/her subject matter boring quickly convinces the students that it is. The teacher who thinks the process of research is an exciting journey often sends students on the same route.

Personality Characteristics

Finally, the personal traits of the teacher must be examined. Those most often considered important by students are enthusiasm, warmth and caring, fairness, and flexibility. At first glance, these qualities may seem to be fixed parts of a personality. After all, can someone who is bored, cold, unfair, or inflexible change? Perhaps not totally. The librarian who is truly bored with the subject matter or actually dislikes students or derives satisfaction from treating students unfairly must change a mental attitude, it would seem, in order to improve.

However, student perceptions of these qualities depend on the behaviors exhibited by the instructor. An interesting series of studies on enthusiasm illustrates the importance of these behaviors.

Mary L. Collins (*Practical Applications of Research,* 1981) developed a list of behaviors which people agreed that enthusiastic instructors demonstrated. The enthusiastic teacher was described as one who has a vocal delivery which varies widely in pitch, volume, and speed; uses large, sweeping gestures; moves freely and sometimes quickly around the room; shows many different facial expressions; has eyes which "light up"; uses many adjectives; reacts strongly when students respond (for example, nods head vigorously in agreement); and appears to be highly energetic. Note that many of these behaviors are mentioned when we talk of good presentation skills.

In contrast, the nonenthusiastic (or boring) instructor was described as one who speaks in a monotone, avoids eye contact, seldom moves the arms or body, rarely smiles, ignores students, and appears lethargic.

Collins developed a scale using these behaviors. Teachers were videotaped, then they were rated according to the scale. Teachers were then encouraged to work on those behaviors on which they were rated low. Subsequent ratings indicated that student rating of the teachers' enthusiasm did indeed rise, even though only the teachers' behavior, not the attitude, changed.

A similar analysis of "warmth and caring" can indicate those behaviors that express these attitudes. What do we mean when we describe a teacher as warm? Some behaviors which come to mind include knowing students' names, smiling when encountering students, and remembering details of the projects they're working on.

Seldom does anyone think of him/herself as being unfair. However, students often describe teachers as "unfair" when they do not know the basis on which they are being evaluated. The course syllabus should make clear what the criteria for evaluation will be. In addition, you should set clear criteria for grading each assignment or test and follow them. These criteria should be shared with the students, preferably when the assignment is made.

Behaviorists feel that changing the behavior of people also changes their attitudes, just as Anna in *The King and I* believed that whistling a happy tune made her unafraid. You may not agree that acting more enthusiastic will lead a teacher to become more enthusiastic about the subject matter. However, students will certainly perceive the instructor as more enthusiastic and more interesting if enthusiastic behaviors are used and practiced.

STUDENT CHARACTERISTICS

Just as the teacher brings certain characteristics to the class-room, so too do students. Very seldom can librarians choose those students they wish to have; instead, they must work with those they receive. Learning about the characteristics of our particular students gives us the information we need to plan the best learning environment possible.

Previous Knowledge and Skills

Most college students will have had varied experiences with libraries. They may come from wealthy school districts with well-supported libraries and may have been frequent users of public libraries. Others may come from inner-city schools or very small rural districts in which a library is nothing more than a corner of a study hall. Older returning students may not have used a library of any kind for years. Librarians have been surprised to discover that students in their third or fourth year at the same college do not know where the periodicals are or how to check out a book.

A first step in determining students' previous knowledge should be a pretest, preferably ungraded to ensure honest student answers rather than guesses, that will give the instructor a clear idea of what the students already know (and don't know). The test should cover what the librarian considers to be the prerequisites for the course. Depending on the students and the level of the course, these prerequisites may range from alphabetizing to assuming basic knowledge of the card catalog or more. The test should also cover some of the objectives of the course, so that the librarian knows whether students can already perform the course content. (See Chapter 6, "Using Evaluation in the Library Course," for specific information on developing a pretest.)

Ability

Obviously, the intellectual ability of the students in every col-lege class varies. However, the ability to do abstract reasoning and to conceptualize varies even more. Both Piaget's theory of devel-opment and the Perry model of intellectual development, the latter currently much discussed in higher education, state that not until an average age of 18 do people acquire the ability to do abstract reasoning. Note that this is an average age: some students reach it sooner, while some never do.

Following these models, we can assume that in a typical freshman class, there will be many students who will have trouble grasping complex abstractions—not because they're not smart enough or don't try, but because they have not yet reached that stage of intellectual development. Understanding this helps the teacher realize the importance of using analogies and a meaningful structure to make concepts clear.

Motivation

There are many reasons why students may be taking a library course. If the course is required, students may resent being there. Even when the course is an elective one, students may be in it for less than desirable reasons: they may view it as a "cake" course, it may be the only thing offered when they need a course, or they may be simply accompanying a friend. In all of these instances, the teacher must demonstrate the value of the course and the importance of taking it.

The most obvious value of a credit course to students is that taking it will help them in their other courses. As librarians, we know that the class should be of lasting value, because it offers students the key to independent learning for the rest of their lives. However, we will be most successful in convincing them that the course is valuable if we show them how what they learn will help them in other classes, or in graduate school, or in applying for a job.

The teacher demonstrates this value by pointing out how various tools and methods learned can be used for other assignments, by telling of previous students who found the course useful, and by designing assignments that pose problems similar to those the students will face elsewhere. For example, an assignment popular with those in every major involves asking students to assume that they're applying for a job with a company and to research that company. Some librarians then have students research the community in which they might live. This is an assignment which is enjoyable, relevant, *and* leads the class to using many different reference books.

Even as we consider ways to motivate students, we must also consider the distractions they are dealing with. Students do not come to class alone. They come with the burdens of the skipped breakfast, the test that went badly the hour before, the fight with a friend, the worries of financing an education, problems with addictions. Any such inner distractions interfere with learning. There is little we can do to avoid them, except to recognize that they will always be there. But we should recognize the possibility that if a student is having trouble with the class, there may well be other reasons besides our teaching technique.

Other kinds of distractions can be dealt with, however. If at all possible, early morning classes should be avoided, as this time seems to be the most undesirable part of the day for most people. Classrooms should be at a comfortable temperature, with comfortable chairs and reasonable insulation from outside noise. A workable classroom is something a teacher should be willing to fight for.

THE PROCESS OF INSTRUCTION

Those involved in product-process research believe that the activities which occur in the classroom are as important in learning as the characteristics of the teacher. There is a considerable amount of research that indicates those things which a teacher can do in order to increase learning.

Organization

Information must be presented within a meaningful structure which makes sense to the student and which ties in to what s/he already knows. Most of us have had an instructor at one time or another who came to class each day and rambled, perhaps in an interesting way, with numerous amusing anecdotes and unusual facts. However, students seldom feel that they are learning anything from such an instructor, and probably they are not.

The teacher who goes through the process of clearly thinking out goals and objectives and selecting an appropriate model has completed the first steps in creating a meaningful structure. However, the teacher should also share these goals and objectives with the students and then make sure that the stated goals are actually what's being taught. Some good instructors begin every class period by stating the goals that are planned to be met that day and why these goals are important both to the course and to the students.

Next, ways of structuring the content so that it makes sense to the students need to be considered. For example, a technique often used in library instruction is that of "walking" students through a search strategy. The instructor chooses a topic of general interest to students, shows an overview article (on a handout or transparency) dealing with the topic, and demonstrates how subtopics or points of view can be identified. Library of Congress subject headings for the narrowed topic are then selected. Finally, the treatment of the topic in several different indexes can be shown. When a student sees how an actual topic should be treated, then the process begins to make sense.

Teaching the use of *I.S.I.* citation indexes can illustrate the importance of organization and building upon what students know. Trying to introduce these indexes by explaining the concept of a citation indexing often results in complete confusion. An analysis of the difficulties reveals 2 problems: the forbidding format of the indexes and the fact that citation indexing is a completely foreign concept to most students.

A better way is to first give students experience in using the "Permuterm" subject part of the indexes. Using indexes to look up a subject is a familiar process; using a "Permuterm" index is just a slightly different way of approaching a subject. Lead them through the process, going from the "Permuterm" index to the source index. Once they have mastered the mechanics of the set, then they're ready for the concept of citation indexing.

Choose a famous figure, such as Freud. He is a good choice, since even nonpsychologists are familiar with him, and he appears in every issue of both *Science Citation Index* and *Social Sciences Citation Index*. (*Interpretation of Dreams* is an appropriate work.) Ask students if it seems reasonable that someone presently doing work in the area of dream analysis would cite Freud in a bibliography. Then ask them to look up Freud in the citation section. The rest of the mechanics come easily, since they are already familiar with them. End by discussing other uses of the citation concept. This approach makes sense to most students. While they may forget the intricacies of the indexes, they will remember that they're manageable and that they have a purpose.

Another example of providing a meaningful structure is one that a librarian uses to demonstrate the relationship between subject headings. S/he makes for each student a packet (reusable) of individual pages from LCSH which shows every single way that "see" and "see also" references can be traced. In this way, the students begin to sense the interconnections. Their assignment is then to create a card for each subject heading which relates to their topic, look the subjects up in the catalog, add call numbers, check shelves or shelf list under that number, and look at the books on either side. If there are new books not previously located, the students go back to the catalog, look them up, check tracings, and follow this procedure until no new books are located. In this way, students realize that subject cataloging is a system—a system which they can control and manipulate.

Student Involvement

While straight lecturing can be an effective way of imparting information and, in very large classes, may be the only feasible method, students tend to remember better if they play an active role in the teaching/learning process. At the most basic level, students should always be asked if they have questions, and the teacher should always respond to student questions.

The instructor's response to questions is important. Remarks such as "That's a good question," or "I'm glad you asked that, it brings up an important point" encourage students to ask further questions. Referring to the question later ("As Amy brought up earlier...") also reinforces questions.

Also important is the way teachers ask questions. Beginning a question with a student's name ("Mark, could you summarize . . .") means that every student except Mark ceases to pay attention. Also, if the teacher's intent is to stimulate discussion, then the questions asked should not be ones that have only one correct answer but, rather, should be ones that are controversial or can be answered in a number of different ways. Asking "How would a sociologist study this topic?" is more likely to elicit discussion than asking someone to define a word. And if you ask a question, then answer it yourself, students will quickly be conditioned never to answer.

Many library instructors feel that the subject matter they teach does not lend itself to discussion. How, they say, can one get students to talk about correct bibliographic format? Yet even in a course which emphasizes skill acquisition, it is possible to elicit discussion.

Start by posing a problem. For example, in the area of topic selection, one might start with a topic of general interest to college students, such as the murder of John Lennon. The teacher may ask how different disciplines might approach studying this event: sociologists might be interested in why our society produces murderers, psychologists in the motivation of Mark David Chapman, market researchers in the impact of the shooting on Beatles record sales.

Have students compare materials. The teacher could distribute copies of a general magazine (such as *Time*), a specialized magazine (*Psychology Today* or *Fortune*), and a professional journal (*Journal of Abnormal Psychology* or *Journal of Marketing*) and ask students to compare and contrast them. They will immediately note the difference in layout and advertising, and with a little jogging, the difference in authors, bibliographies, and use of evidence. Beaubien gives numerous other examples of methods of sparking discussion (1982).

Thomas P. Kasaulis (1982), in a good discussion of questioning techniques, suggests that responses to questions can be improved by giving students some guidelines for their answers. The teacher may set limits: "In a few words, could you...," "If you had to pick one thing..."; or give instruction as to the level of abstraction: "Can you give specific examples...?," "If you were to generalize ..." He favors students being asked to summarize a discussion or a class in order to avoid the teacher always being in control.

Finally, the arrangement of the classroom can facilitate or discourage discussion. The traditional classroom—teacher standing in front at a desk or lectern, students in rows all facing the teacher—directs all attention to the teacher. Rearranging desks or tables in a circle so that students are facing other students makes interaction more possible. If the instructor also sits in the circle, then students are most likely to discuss among themselves. If the teacher then wants to reassume control, standing up will immediately bring everyone's attention back to the instructor.

Practice and Transfer

Good teaching also allows for student practice and transfer of the skills they are supposed to learn. Nearly all library credit courses require the completion of exercises and assignments that ask students to demonstrate skills. Few of us would attempt to teach students library skills only by telling them, just as we would avoid teaching swimming by lecture only.

As discussed in the previous chapter, careful construction of assignments is necessary in order to ensure that students practice more than just low-level skills and that they learn that skills are transferable. We want students to be able not just to do what is required in one class but also to use these skills in later situations.

Use of Media

There is ample evidence to support the contention that the use of more than one medium promotes learning. Students retain information better when more than one sense is involved. Good teachers consistently help students understand the organization of a lesson by highlighting points on a chalkboard, an overhead projector, or on handouts. Illustrating a search strategy by making a flowchart helps students understand a strategy as a process. Showing actual objects—a book or a page from an index—or a picture of the object ensures that the students know what is being talked about.

Classroom Dynamics

The relationships between the characteristics of the teacher and those of the students and the process of instruction form the dynamics of the classroom. We can often sense the dynamics by just walking into a class: whether the students are involved and interested in the class and whether they consider it important. All of the factors discussed in this chapter contribute to the feeling in the classroom. Effective teaching and learning is not a simple process but a complex, interactive one with many variables.

Using the checklist which follows can help to identify those variables which need strengthening. A typical reaction to a list like this is to check off those things that one does, and to feel good about those, and to consider the items not checked off as not worth the effort to do. However, each item on the list is one that many effective teachers consider important to do.

CHECKLIST FOR DEVELOPING EFFECTIVE TEACHING TECHNIQUES

- Establish clear goals and objectives for the course.
- Share the goals and objectives with the students.
- Demonstrate to students why meeting these goals is important to them.
- Create exercises and assignments that require students to apply the desired skills.
- Plan the first day of class carefully; you only have one chance to make a first impression.
- Pretest students to determine their level of knowledge and skills at the beginning of the course.
- Acquire other pertinent information about the students: majors, interests, classes which require library work.
- Learn students' names as soon as possible.
- Have a trusted colleague sit in on a class to give feedback on presentation skills.
- Practice on willing nonlibrarians the explanation of unique library concepts.
- Arrange the classroom physically to optimize learning and interaction.
- Ask students for feedback on presentations, assignments, and worth of class.
- Have clearly stated criteria for grading, share these criteria with students, and follow them.
- Experiment with questioning techniques.
- Choose one teaching skill (presentation or classroom process method) to work on each term.

REFERENCES

Beaubien, A.K., Hogan, S., and George, M. (1982). *Learning the library.* New York, Bowker.

Brophy, J.E. (1979). *Advances in teacher effectiveness research.* Bethesda, MD: ERIC Document Reproduction Service (ED 173 340).

Centra, J.A. (1981). *Determining faculty effectiveness.* San Francisco, CA: Jossey-Bass.

Kasaulis, T.P. (1982). Questioning. In M. Gullette (Ed.), *The art and craft of teaching* (pp. 38–48). Cambridge, MA: Harvard-Danforth Center for Teaching and Learning.

Practical applications for research, 3 (1), June 1981.

Ramagli, H.A., and Greenwood, G. (1980). *The Doctor Fox effect.* Bethesda, MD: ERIC Document Reproduction Service (ED 187 179).

Wallechinsky, D., et al. (1977). *The book of lists.* New York: William Morrow.

Wotruba, T.R., and Wright, P.L. (1975). How to develop a teaching-rating instrument. *Journal of higher education, 46,* 653–663.

FOR FURTHER READING

Beaubien, A.K., Hogan, S.A., and George, M.W. (1982). *Learning the library: Concepts and methods for effective bibliographic instruction.* New York: Bowker.
Presents numerous examples, including methods of organization and descriptions of sample classes.

Eble, K.E. (1977). *The craft of teaching.* San Francisco, CA: Jossey-Bass.
Presents college teaching as an art, rather than a science. Particularly helpful is Chapter 4, "Making Classes Work."

Fuhrmann, B.S., and Grasha, A.F. (1983). *A practical handbook for college teachers.* Boston: Little, Brown & Co.
An excellent and clear presentation of major theories of teaching and learning (not necessarily the same thing). The last chapters consider aspects of teaching, course design, and use of media.

Jay, H.L. (1983). *Stimulating student search: Library media/ classroom teacher techniques.* Hamden, CO: Library Professional Publications.
Although aimed at school librarians, the book has useful ideas for college librarians for teaching topic selection and organizing searches. The last half of the book contains sample assignments.

McKeachie, W.J. (1978). *Teaching tips: A guidebook for the beginning college teacher.* (7th ed.). Lexington, MA: D.C. Heath.
McKeachie is a psychologist noted for his studies on effective college teaching. This book is a blend of the theoretical and practical aspects of teaching, from learning theory to buttering up librarians. Everyone can learn from McKeachie.

Mellon, C.A., and Sass, E. (May 1981). Perry and Piaget: Theoretical framework for effective college course development. *Educational Technology,* pp. 29–33.

A look at how the models of Perry and Piaget relate to the teaching of college students. Suggested methods are given to encourage students to move from concrete reasoning/dualistic stages to higher ones.

Perry, W.G. (1968). *Forms of intellectual and ethical development in the college years: A scheme.* Cambridge, MA: Harvard College.

Explanation of the longitudinal study which led Perry to develop his model. Includes examples of stages, as well as a discussion of their educational implications.

Chapter 6:
Evaluation and the Library Course

Evaluation refers to the gathering of data in a systematic manner in order to make decisions. Evaluation techniques can be used to gather information about students entering the course, so that the instructor knows at what level they are at, to gain feedback from students at the end of the course in order to improve the course in the future, or to compile data in order to demonstrate the effectiveness of the course. However, the most commonly used evaluation technique in college courses is the test, used in order to determine the assignment of grades to students (or to decide which students pass and which fail). Tests, as well as any other evaluative measure, should be derived from objectives, so that they measure what they were actually intended to.

PRETESTING

In order to teach effectively, you should be aware of what your students already know and can do. Most librarians do not have a clear idea of what students already know about libraries and library use. Their assumptions are based on questions received at the reference desk, and a typical conclusion is that students know nothing. Since we are more likely to receive, and certainly most likely to notice, the clearly naive questions, we forget that many library users go directly, quietly, and proficiently about their business. Pretests are a way to find out what students already know, so that covering familiar territory is avoided. Pretesting is also a way of identifying students who do not meet the prerequisites. For an upper-level course, you may want to assume attainment of basic skills. A pretest will reveal those students who cannot identify a call number or interpret an index citation. They can be referred to one of the basic library textbooks or come to an extra instructional session. You do not want to bore the proficient students with redundant information.

A pretest can also serve as a confirmation to students that the course will cover material they do not know. Many students have had instruction in library use in elementary school, junior high, and high school. So they may feel that there is little to learn, especially when they take the course as a requirement rather than a choice. Difficult questions convince them that they do not know it all already, and such a realization may increase their motivation.

Finally, whether or not you give a pretest, you will probably want some background information from your students, such as a major, year in school, and local address. Other information, such as how the students discovered the course, will help in marketing it.

Following is an example of a pretest for an upper-level course, whose assumed prerequisites are that students can interpret a catalog card, locate a book on the shelves, and interpret an index entry. The final questions come from the objectives of the course.

Example of a Pretest

PERSONAL BACKGROUND
Name:
Local address and phone:
Major:
Year in school:
Are you taking a course this semester in which you expect to write a research paper? If so, what course (the name, please)?
How did you find out about this course (Library Research Techniques)?
What do you hope to gain from taking this course?
PRETEST
You will not be graded on this test. Do not guess.
1. Items on a catalog card.
(This item shows an illustration of a catalog card and asks students to pick out the call number, bibliographic notes, author, date of publication, title, and tracings.)
2. Interpreting an index entry.
(This item shows an illustration of an entry from the *Readers' Guide* and asks students to identify the author, title of the article, title of the periodical, volume number, pages, and date.)

Example of a Pretest (continued)

---

3. Finding books.
   Tell what you would use from the catalog card in question 1 to find this book on the shelf; tell how you would go about finding it and what you would do if it were not on the shelf.
4. Name a specialized index or abstracting service which indexes periodicals related to your major.
Major:
Index or abstract:
5. You have been assigned a paper on some aspect of computer-assisted instruction. Outline the steps you would take in researching this topic, including finding enough information to define and limit the topic; mention particular sources you would use.

Another type of pretest sometimes used in library courses is a performance measure. For example, students may be asked to conduct a minisearch strategy. Within a given time period, they must, for a given topic, locate a recent book with a bibliography, and choose and use a suitable periodical index to locate a citation. They may also be asked to retrieve the book and article. This kind of pretest is valuable because it asks students to do what you actually want them to be able to do; also, students enjoy the activity, as opposed to passive responding.

EXAMINATIONS

The primary use of testing in library courses is to have a basis for assigning grades or to determine if the student is to receive credit for the course. Assignments alone can provide enough information, but many instructors prefer also to have some kind of test. In addition, if tests are, as they should be, derived from your goals and objectives, you will not only have the basis for student grades, but you'll also know if you taught them what you wanted to.

Tests can be of the pencil-and-paper variety, taken in a room with no recourse to library materials. They can also be performance measures, such as the pretest described in the previous section. What a test must do, however, is measure what you want students to be able to do. If your goal is that students can use certain library tools, then do not test them on the history of the book, but on the use of these tools.

Test items should be written from the course objectives. If the objectives are clear and written in terms of expected student behavior, then writing good test items will be easy. If the objectives are not clear or if they are ignored, then test items like this may be written:

> Reference sources are of 2 main types. One type includes directories, encyclopedias, and dictionaries. What is the other type?

This item tests for the objective: students will be able to list 2 types of reference materials. This objective is probably not what the instructor wanted to teach, since being able to list 2 types of reference materials has little to do with being able to use a library (even if we could all agree on what the 2 types of reference materials are).

However, if you start from a course objective, an objective which you really care whether or not your students can meet, then writing good test items becomes much easier. For example, a course objective might be:

> Students will be able to select appropriate reference tools for their information needs.

This objective can easily be turned into a test question:

> Choose the best reference tool from the following list to find the kind of information described in each item. Place the letter of the tool in the space to the left of each item.
>
> A. Encyclopedia
> B. *Readers' Guide*
> C. *Social Sciences Index*
> D. Almanac
> E. Bibliography
>
> 1. Current information on home uses of personal computers.
> 2. Statistics on crime rates.
> 3. A general idea of what the War of 1812 was about.
> 4. An account of a research study dealing with alcoholics.

Many test items test only for recall of specific information, the lowest level in Bloom's *Taxonomy of Objectives* (Bloom, 1956), as described in Chapter 3, "Planning the Library Course." While students must acquire knowledge, they also need to be able to understand, apply, evaluate—and test items should test not only knowledge of facts, but also these other abilities. While we want students to be able to label parts of a catalog card, most of us also want them to be able to achieve higher objectives; we can test them on whether or not they have.

Multiple-Choice Testing

Multiple-choice tests are the easiest to grade. If you are dealing with large numbers of students, you will be interested in tests that can be scored by computer (or at least with a template to set over the answers). For a very large class, multiple-choice questions are probably the best option.

Many people feel that multiple-choice questions can measure only low-level objectives. However, Bloom's *Taxonomy* has examples of hundreds of multiple-choice questions which measure very high-level objectives. (Unfortunately, none of its examples deal with libraries.) Here are some ways in which multiple-choice questions can be developed from higher objectives:

Objective: Students can select a suitable index to locate relevant articles from professional literature.

Test item: You have found an article which suits your needs in the *Journal of Studies on Alcohol.* Which of these tools should you use to find a similar article?

   A. *Readers' Guide*
   B. *Social Sciences Index*
   C. *Humanities Index*

Objective: Students will recognize the limitations of the card catalog and use alternate strategies to overcome them.

Test item: You cannot find anything in the card catalog under "genetic mutation." Your next step should be to:

   A. Use the Library of Congress list of subject headings to generate additional search terms.
   B. Go to a larger library.
   C. Look for periodical articles, since there are no books on the subject in this library.
   D. Look under "biology."

Good multiple-choice questions take longer to write than other types of test items. However, pretests or proficiency exams can be reused. For classroom examinations, some instructors place good test items on cards, adding some and deleting some each time they give an examination. The test can then be typed from the cards. A microcomputer can also be used to store items, with the added feature that questions can be pulled out at random and several different configurations used in the same testing situation.

True-False Questions

Writing good true-false test items is extremely difficult because of the problem of creating statements which are either completely true or completely false. In addition, unless the student receives immediate feedback, s/he may remember a false statement from the test and assume it is true. For these reasons, many test experts recommend not using a true-false format.

Short-Answer Questions

Short-answer questions require students to supply their own entire answers without the prompts in multiple-choice questions, thus making a guess more difficult. However, this type of test cannot be graded as quickly as multiple-choice questions nor does it require the students to be able to organize their answers as in essay tests.

Because there are fewer clues, wording is important in short-answer questions. For example, if students are asked where they would find certain types of information, they should be told whether they are to respond with the name of a specific source (e.g., *Bioabstract* or a type (e.g., an abstracting service for biology).

Like multiple-choice questions, short-answer questions can test not only for recall of knowledge ("Define the following terms") but also for higher-level objectives ("Fawn Brodie wrote a controversial book about Thomas Jefferson. What would you use to find out quickly the reactions of Jefferson scholars?").

Essay Questions

Essay questions are regarded by test experts as the only type which can test for students' ability to organize their responses. Questions which ask students to demonstrate mastery of higher-level objectives are much easier to write in essay form than in multiple choice form. However, even using the techniques described later, grading essay examinations take far more time than multiple-choice and may not be a viable choice for testing large numbers of students. Essay questions can be constructed to test only one objective, such as the following:

Objective: Students will recognize the limitations of the card catalog and be able to develop alternative ways of overcoming the limitations.

Test item: You have been assigned a paper on genetic mutation for your biology class. You go to the library and look under "genetic mutation" in the card catalog. Nothing is there. Does this mean the library has no books on the topic? What should be your next step?

Essay questions can also be designed to test a number of different objectives. For example, the following test item covers objectives ranging from card catalog use to search strategy to evaluation of materials.

Test item: Your roommate has been working on a paper for a psychology class. Following is the preliminary report turned in to the psychology instructor. Since you have been taking a course in library research, your roommate has asked you to criticize this report in terms of topic chosen, search method used, and quality of its bibliography. What should your roommate do differently in order to research the paper adequately?

"Psych 300 Paper: Drug Use among College Students"

I checked the card catalog under "drugs." Only a couple of books were listed that looked good, and they were checked out. So, the following bibliography is all periodical articles.
"Drugs and the Generation Gap." *McCall's,* September 1969, pp. 35–36.
"College Students: What Are They Doing?" *Time,* October 14, 1970, p. 81.
"Marijuana Use Rising." *Newsweek,* February 10, 1970, p. 23.
"Caffeine, Alcohol, and Nicotine." *Vogue,* August 1969, pp. 13–15. (The library doesn't have this one; I'll check the public library next week if I can borrow a car.)

Library course students answering this question point out that the topic is much too broad, alternative subject headings should have been used, and articles are too old and from magazines written for general readers. They recommend using the search strategy they've been taught, and point out that interlibrary loan doesn't depend on a car.

While essay tests do take longer to grade than multiple-choice, these procedures can make the process somewhat faster:

- Write the essay question from the course objectives.
- Decide if organization and/or writing style will be part of the grade.
- Make a list of points that you're looking for in each question.
- Read through all of the answers to the first question and grade them, then through all of the answers to the second, and so on, rather than grading each student's entire test, one at a time. This will make your grading more consistent as well as faster.
- Make a check mark next to each point covered.
- Count up the check marks to see what the score for the question should be.

Performance Measures

Performance measures are a more accurate way of determining what students will do in a real situation, not just what they say they would do. The pretest described earlier, which asks students to go through a search strategy for a given topic, is a performance measure. Some other examples of performance measures are these:

- Select groups of 5 or 10 books, roughly on the same topic. Have students evaluate and rank them as to their credibility, based on evidence within the book and/or the use of reviews.
- Choose articles from a general magazine and a professional journal and have students compare them. (These could be photocopies, or old copies of periodicals could be used, or students could be sent to find them.)

The above examples could, of course, be assignments (and many library assignments are performance measures). However, they become test items if you set the situations up with a time limit and do not allow students to obtain help from either classmates or librarians.

Performance measures are valid testing devices and can often reveal students' abilities to perform rather than describe. However, requiring a performance measure as a test produces anxiety in many students, particularly those who are extremely grade-conscious. They do not feel that they know how to study or otherwise prepare for them.

Take-home exams, which often contain some performance measures on them, also create anxiety in many students. They are always unsure as to how much time they should spend on them, and some students will spend an exorbitant amount of time on them. For both performance measures and take-home exams, instructors need to carefully set limits as to what is expected. Otherwise, students' anxiety may well interfere with their ability to perform.

ASSIGNING GRADES

Librarians are often uncomfortable with the process of assigning grades. We are trained to be, and in most of our work situations are, sympathetic, helpful, and supportive; we want to encourage library use. Most of us would prefer to give all our students "A's." However, unless the library course is a component of another course in which someone else assigns the grades, the process of labeling students is a necessary duty, one which is required in most academic situations.

Students are very concerned about the criteria used for grading. In order to be perceived as fair, you should be as specific as possible, and as soon as possible. It is best if grading criteria are included on the syllabus.

In courses where the requirements are 2 exams and a paper, grading is fairly simple. The instructor can average the grades. However, library courses often have a number of assignments, perhaps one large project, and possibly an examination. The first step in establishing criteria is to decide what weight each of these components should have. If attendance is required, you may want to include that within the weighting. For example, you may decide that the project should be 40 percent of the final grade, assignments 30 percent, examinations 25 percent, and attendance 5 percent.

You may want to assign grades on each component and indicate how much of the total each one is. However, a simpler way is to set an arbitrary number of points and assign a proportionate amount of points to each component. For example:

10 assignments at 6 points each	60 points
research project	80
examinations	50
attendance	10
	200 total

The total number of points should depend on the number of individual items which will carry points. If, for instance, you had only 4 assignments and an exam, then 50 or 100 points would be sufficient. If the example above, however, were based on 100 points, the assignments could be worth only 3 points apiece, giving you little room to maneuver in grading unless you resort to half or quarter points.

Expressing grades in numbers creates a feeling of objectivity. In reality, the process of assigning numbers is as subjective as assigning letter grades. Numbers can also be somewhat misleading. If assignments are fill-in-the-blank worksheets, which students easily do by following directions, this means that nearly all students receive the same number of points for the worksheets. The result is that other items (the test or research project) may by themselves determine who receives what grades. If you have assigned only a small number of points to these items, your grading range will be quite small. Be aware of this and do not assign a great deal of weight to items for which almost everyone will get full credit. Another way to assign grades is to set expected levels of achievement. For example:

A= all assignments completed satisfactorily *and* average grade on tests and project B+ or above

B= all assignments completed satisfactorily *and* average grades no lower than C+

C= all but one or 2 completed satisfactorily *and* average grades no lower than C

D= all but 3 or 4 completed satisfactorily *and* average grades no lower than D

E= 5 or more not completed satisfactorily *and* average grades D or lower

Still another way to deal with grading is to use a contract method. In this method, each grade carries certain requirements and students are asked to select (or "contract" for) the grade they want. For example:

A = satisfactory completion of assignments; lengthy research project

B = satisfactory completion of assignments; short research project

C = satisfactory completion of assignments

Theoretically, students select their level, and the instructor is freed from much of the decision making surrounding grades. In practice, most students will contract for an "A."

Pass/fail courses obviate some of the problems of grading. However, does the student with a 97 as well as the one with 65 both pass, while the student with a 64 fails? Students seldom fall neatly into satisfactory or unsatisfactory categories. Even pass/fail courses often require some unpleasant decision making.

COURSE EVALUATION

If assignments and tests have been designed to measure course objectives, then you will have a good idea if the course is fulfilling its purpose. However, there are other questions which you will probably want answers to. Did students find the course worthwhile? What needs to be changed? What assignments could be improved? Answers to these kinds of questions require evaluative measures other than tests.

Student Evaluation

Obtaining student reactions at the end of the course gives feedback on the strengths and weaknesses of it, ideas for improvement, and a feeling of the worth of the course. Some colleges have a standard questionnaire (sometimes required for all instructors) which can be computer-scored. Occasionally, the statistical program for these questionnaires includes comparison with other courses. Use such a form if one is available, but even if it is, you may want to administer a questionnaire of your own making which will answer your own questions. You might want to ask students these questions:

● Did the students find the course worthwhile?
● Did they learn from it?

- Did they learn what they wanted to learn?
- Were the assignments helpful in learning?
- What about the instructor's presentation? Was s/he clear, enthusiastic, a good deliverer?
- Was the instructor helpful? Did s/he seem to care about students?
- Were the course requirements clear?
- Was the work load appropriate for the credit received, neither too much nor too little?
- What were the best features of the class? The worst?
- What could be done to make the course better?

Being evaluated by students can be scary. However, student responses tend to be higher than the instructor expects, and there is a great deal of useful information which can be obtained. The information should belong to the instructor, to do with as s/he sees fit.

For information to be useful, you should encourage students to be as honest as possible. Some instructors have been known to bring cookies to class, pass out the evaluation form, tell students that their handwriting is recognizable, and that the evaluations will affect the instructor's job. They then walk around the room looking at what the students are writing. Any or all of these procedures may reduce the instructor's stress, but the responses will yield little useful information. Techniques for administering a student evaluation include the following:

- There should be no threat that a student's response will in any way affect a grade. Therefore, students should be asked not to sign their names. A multiple-choice format which requires no recognizable handwriting produces the most honest responses. However, open-ended questions can also provide valuable input; they should go on another sheet of paper.
- Ideally, the evaluation form should be completed by students with the teacher absent. In any case, the instructor should not collect the forms. One way to meet these requirements is to pass out the forms at the end of class, place on a table an envelope or folder for the completed forms, and leave the room.
- Probably due to anxiety, students tend to rate a class lower if they complete the forms at the same time they take an

examination. The last day of regular class is perhaps a better time to pass out evaluation forms.

- Recognize that many factors can affect responses. Students tend to rate elective courses higher than required, upper-level higher than lower-level, and younger teachers higher than older ones.
- Include open-ended questions; they usually give much useful information.
- Disregard the one or 2 most positive comments and the one or 2 most negative. You are interested in the general reaction of the class. It is human nature to remember poor comments. If there are a hundred glowing responses and one terribly negative one, it is that one which will be engraved on a teacher's soul. However, even the best teachers may have personality clashes with one or 2 students. Look at the typical responses for a better idea of the total class response.

Along with student evaluations, you may also want to solicit information from your colleagues who work at the reference desk. They can note if there are assignments which are giving students difficulty. In addition, if they feel that they are involved, their attitude toward the course is likely to be more positive.

DEMONSTRATING THE EFFECTIVENESS OF THE COURSE

Most of the information that we need in order to improve the teaching of a course, or its content and structure, can be obtained from feedback on assignments, student comments, or peer evaluation. However, as is true for library instruction in general, librarians often feel that library courses need to be justified. Are they worth the time? Do they make any lasting impact on students?

Other college courses seldom have to be defended in this fashion. If students enroll in them, if students and departments feel the courses are worthwhile, then their existence is not questioned. Because library instruction is a relatively recent addition to library services (and diverts resources from other services), it is often necessary for librarians to provide documentation that this instruction is indeed valuable. In this case, more formal evaluation techniques may provide answers.

Begin by considering the purpose of the evaluation. You may want to determine that the course met its objectives, which probably means that the course improved students' knowledge and skills. Or you may want to show that students' behaviors changed, so that they now use libraries differently. Student attitudes and perceptions of the course may also be important. Each of these purposes implies a different evaluative technique and instrument.

Have Students' Skills Improved?

Demonstrating an improvement in student knowledge and skills requires comparison (improved over what?). This can be done either by comparing students at the beginning and end of the course through a pre- and posttest or by comparing test results of students who have taken the course with those of students who have not.

The latter comparison can demonstrate that any improvement in skills is due to the course and not to other experiences the students may have had. For example, a study at Slippery Rock University (Wood, 1984) compared 40 students enrolled in a freshman library course with 46 randomly chosen freshmen. Each group completed library skills pre- and posttests and an attitude survey. The course enrollees showed significant improvement both in learning skills and attitude, thus demonstrating the effectiveness of the course.

Have Students' Behaviors Changed?

You may wish to demonstrate that taking the library course alters the way in which students go about using the library. A performance test which compares students from the course with non-course takers might be one way to show this, but such a test can be difficult and time-consuming to set up. Another way might be to locate a subsequent course and compare the bibliographies written by your former students with those of other students. You could also ask the instructor for feedback or to have his/her students describe how they went about pursuing their research.

Librarians often use observation to conclude that student behaviors have changed. They may notice former students working in the library or assisting friends in research projects.

However, observation can lead to invalid conclusions. We often notice what we want to notice and remember what we want to remember. To be more systematic, you might try keeping a log handy and jotting down a brief description of each interaction with a former student. Such a log will not tell you whether or how your students have changed (because there is no comparison involved), but you will have anecdotal information which may be helpful.

How Do Students Feel About the Course?

Student perceptions of the course and its value can be useful documentation. In addition to student evaluation forms completed at the end of a course, follow-up surveys can be used. A follow-up survey with an adequate response rate can provide you with information as to whether the students feel the library course was useful in later course work and whether they continue to feel that the course is worthwhile. Favorable results from such a survey can furnish excellent evidence that students feel the course met its objectives.

Using Campus Resources

On any college campus, there are faculty members who have expertise in research design, testing, and questionnaire construction. Use the resources which are available to you in order to create evaluation designs and instruments which will be valid. Look for faculty members in education, psychology, and sociology who teach courses in research methodology, statistics, or evaluation. An hour spent with an expert reviewing your approach and instruments can save you hours of fumbling and help to ensure that you have information you can use.

Once you have obtained information, make sure that it is shared with those who are influential about the future of the course. For an elective course, these people would include the library director, other librarians, and faculty advisors. For a required course, make sure that deans and other concerned administrators know what the course's strengths are. If many influential people are aware that the course is effective or that students regard it highly, then the course will continue to have the support it needs.

SUMMARY

Course instructors most often use evaluation techniques in order to create tests. However, teacher-made tests are often poor. Tests can be improved if they are always derived from course objectives, so that they measure what was intended to be taught. Tests can also be constructed which ask students to demonstrate more than just recall of facts.

Evaluation techniques can also be used to gather valuable information both to improve the course in the future and to ascertain whether students benefitted from the course. Systematic evaluation and the distribution of the evaluation's results can help to ensure that others recognize the value of the course. Documenting the course's effectiveness is the best way to make sure that the course can continue.

REFERENCES

Bloom, B. (1956). *Taxonomy of educational objectives. Vol. I: The cognitive domain.* Chicago: David McKay.

Wood, R.J. (1984). The impact of a library research course on students at Slippery Rock University. *Journal of Academic Librarianship, 10,* 278–284.

FOR FURTHER READING

Association of College and Research Libraries. Bibliographic Instruction Section. (1983). *Evaluating Bibliographic Instruction.* Chicago: American Library Association.
Designed as an introduction to evaluation theory and techniques for librarians. Contains chapters on goals and objectives, research design, data-gathering instruments, and statistics.

Centra, J.A. (1981). *Determining Faculty Effectiveness.* San Francisco, CA: Jossey-Bass.
Contains an appendix of commercially available student evaluation forms.

Knapp, P. (1966). *The Montieth College library experiment.* Metuchen, NJ: Scarecrow Press.

> Chapter 4 describes an extensive performance measure developed to measure library skills.

McKeachie, W.J. (1978). *Teaching tips.* Lexington, MA: D.C. Heath.

> Of particular value are Chapter 16, "Examinations"; Chapter 17, "The ABC's of Assigning Grades"; and Chapter 26, "Student Rating of Faculty." An appendix contains a student evaluation form, which teachers are free to copy and use with classes.

Payne, S.L. (1951). *The art of asking questions.* Princeton, NJ: Princeton University Press.

> Although over 30 years old, this is still the most readable and sensible guide to the good wording of questions.

There are a number of basic texts which serve as good guides to test construction. Among these are:

Ebel, R.L. (1979). *Essentials of educational measurement.* (3rd ed.). Englewood Cliffs, NJ: Prentice-Hall.

Gronlund, N.E. (1981). *Measurement and evaluation in teaching.* (4th ed.). New York: Macmillan.

Lien, A.J. (1980). *Measurement and evaluation of learning.* (4th ed.). Dubuque, IA: W.C. Brown.

Texts on survey research which discuss the writing of questionnaires include:

Backstrom, C.H. (1963). *Survey research.* Evanston, IL: Northwestern University Press.

Oppenheim, A.N. (1966). *Questionnaire design and attitude measurement.* New York: Basic Books.

Pope, J.L. (1981). *Practical marketing and research.* New York: AMACOM.

Part II Case Studies

About the Case Studies

This section contains descriptions of 18 library courses taught at institutions around the country. They were chosen because of the variety of classes they represent: freshmen and graduate levels, general and subject-specific, required and elective, lecture and independent study. Some have been spectacularly successful. Others illustrate some of the problems that can beset library courses: difficulties in gaining approval on a local campus or in attracting enrollment. For various reasons, 2 have not yet been taught as credit courses.

The contributors to this section were asked to describe their courses, including any problems or solutions they wish they'd known about before they started. Their answers are various. One writer felt that the philosophy of teaching which has evolved for her class was the most important advice that she could pass on. Many expressed their feeling that their course is still in a process of growth and change. Anyone presently teaching a class, planning or even hoping to, can find a wealth of ideas and approaches in this section.

Case Study #1: Central Oregon Community College

Library/Media Services
Bend, OR 97701
Margaret C. Mason, Director
Rebecca Thompson, Faculty Librarian

Central Oregon Community College is one of Oregon's 15 2-year colleges which provides lower-division, transfer courses; technical programs; and noncredit community education classes. The 2,100 full- and part-time students are primarily from Oregon and their average age is 26. The library holds approximately 35,000 volumes and 350 journal titles. Its 2 professional librarians participate in the college library skills program.

COURSE DESCRIPTION

Lib 127: College Library Skills is a one-credit-hour class. All students are registered in one section with a to-be-arranged schedule. Students must attend 3 formal class meetings: an introductory meeting held during the first week of classes, a midterm exam held halfway through the term, and a final exam held during finals week. For each of the 3 meetings, 8 to 12 different times are offered and posted; students select a time that fits into their schedule.

In addition to the meetings, students work independently on the course materials at times of their own choosing. Assistance is available, if required, whenever the library is open. Optional review sessions for the midterm and final exam are also held.

The intent of the class is to make students familiar and comfortable with the library early in their college career, so the target population is students in their first or second term. For this reason, students who register in WR 121, the first term in the writing composition sequence, must also register in Lib 127. However, there is no curricular connection between the 2 courses.

BACKGROUND

Library director Margaret Mason approached several of the WR 121 instructors in 1979 about including in their classes a section on use of the library which would be taught by the librarian. Response from most of the instructors was positive, and 2 agreed to try it. The first bibliographic instruction section was about an hour long and consisted of a brief overview of the card catalog and indexes. No assignments were given.

By fall 1980, Mason had written a workbook and again approached all writing instructors about using their classes as a vehicle for teaching library skills, this time using a workbook. A half-hour explanation of the purpose of the course would be given in class and workbooks would be given to students at no charge, to be collected and graded by the librarian. Students were expected to complete the workbook before the end of the term, and grades (pass or fail) would be sent to the instructors who could then decide, on an individual basis, whether to consider the library grade in determining a student's grade for the writing class.

During 1980, a half-time position was budgeted for the following academic year. Rebecca Thompson was employed in the fall of 1981, with her primary responsibilities being to coordinate bibliographic instruction, revise the text, and handle all grading and student contact. The text was rewritten and bibliographic instruction was again administered through the writing classes.

During 1981, this method of instruction was evaluated. Writing instructors supported the concept of library instruction but found it difficult to incorporate it into their tightly scheduled WR 121 classes. The librarians worked together to develop the idea of a one-credit course, separate from WR 121 in terms of grading and content, but linked to it by a registration requirement. The text was revised again, a course description written, and the Instructional Affairs Committee approached for approval. Since the course had been offered on a trial basis for 2 years, the Instructional Affairs Committee (with the strong support of Dr. John Weber, dean of instruction, and Dr. Bart Queary, chair, division of humanities, social sciences and fine arts), approved the proposal. Lib 127 became a separate course in the fall of 1982. At that time, Thompson became a full-time faculty librarian. In the 1982–83 academic year, 610 students enrolled in the course.

MARKETING

Because Lib 127 is required for students who take WR 121, and WR 121 is required for many degree and certification programs, we do not need to market the course. Each term, we have students taking the course as an elective. A number of faculty who assign research papers to their students recommend Lib 127 to their advisees. Students who attend other course-related presentations become aware of the importance of Lib 127 and sometimes enroll in the course at a later date.

COURSE OBJECTIVES

Course objectives for Lib 127 are as follows:

- To introduce students to basic reference materials found in college libraries.
- To develop some skill in using basic reference materials.
- To acquaint students with the resources and services of the COCC library.

Course Outline

   I.   The card catalog
       A. Information on a catalog card
       B. Filing rules
       C. *Library of Congress Subject Headings List*
  II. Ready reference materials
 III. Indexes
       A. Periodical indexes
       B. Newspaper indexes
       C. Other indexes (play, poetry, etc.)

IV. Special Collections and Services
   A. Government documents
   B. Online searching
   C. Oregon Collection
   D. Media services

COURSE REQUIREMENTS

Students work through course materials independently at times of their own choosing. The course materials are in 2 parts: a text with basic information and an exercise book which supplies hands-on experience.

Students are not required to complete the workbook or turn it in. Answer keys are available for the students to check their own work. This procedure serves 3 purposes. First, students come to class with a variety of library experiences. No student is required to complete an exercise on material already learned, and thus any perception of busy work is eliminated. Second, the fact that exercise books are not graded discourages copying. Students know that copying is not going to help them learn the material. Third, because of the large enrollment (close to 300 students for the fall term), our small staff could not possibly correct all of the exercise books.

Course materials are revised annually to cope with changes and with problems encountered by students in using the materials. Four versions of the exercise book have been printed to alleviate potential simultaneous demand and/or abuse of certain materials through overuse.

Students are evaluated on the basis of their scores on a midterm and final exam, which contain objective, short-answer items.The tests are designed to demonstrate knowledge of and ability to use basic types of reference materials. For the first 2 years of the class, all students were graded on a pass/unsatisfactory basis. Beginning in the fall of 1984, letter grading was instituted for all students enrolled in the course. In addition, all students who finish the course are given an evaluation form to complete. The forms are summarized and tabulated each term.

STRENGTHS AND WEAKNESSES

Major strengths of the course are numerous. A strong institutional commitment has been made to library instruction by the president, dean of instruction, and other administrators and faculty of the college. The concurrent requirement with WR 121 enables us to reach a large number of students who, under other circumstances, might never come into the library. This large number of students is being provided with solid and identifiable basic library skills. In the classes in which we give course-related instruction, we can not only cover more sophisticated research concepts, but we can plan our presentations knowing that most of the audience will already have acquired basic skills.

A major weakness of the course is that limited staffing presents problems. Students may not get as much individual help as they would like. While there is a degree of flexibility in the scheduling, students are still locked into a specific time frame in which to take exams. We are exploring the possibility of putting our tests online with a testing software package for a micro combined with a Caramate slide projector. This would not only enable students to take tests any time during the term but would also automate test correcting and record keeping.

Another drawback is that, for some students, a course that requires independent scheduling is problematic. Students who have difficulty planning their time and meeting long-range deadlines frequently are unprepared for tests. Our staffing limitations dictate that the only regular library instruction we can offer is independent instruction. We feel that the number of students we reach balances out this weakness to some degree. We have also discovered that even students who don't pass Lib 127 may become regular library users and use library resources that are unfamiliar to the average library patron.

Case Study #2: State University of New York College at Plattsburgh

Benjamin F. Feinberg Library
Plattsburgh, NY 12901
Carla List, Administrator of Library Research Skills
Dennis Kimmage, Head, Reference Department

The College at Plattsburgh, an arts and science college within the SUNY system, enrolls about 6,200 students under a competitive admission policy. Most of the students are full-time undergraduates from within the state, many living on campus. The library contains approximately 250,000 volumes and carries about 1,600 periodical subscriptions. There are 17 librarians on the faculty, 11 of whom participate in instruction; 3 to 5 area librarians also serve as instructors on a part-time basis each semester.

COURSE DESCRIPTION

Lib 101: Library Research Skills is a one-credit, required course, offered every semester. It is currently a 7-week course consisting of 7 50-minute lectures and 7 50-minute discussion sections. It is part of the general education requirements which are to be taken before junior standing is achieved. The intended audience is entering freshmen and other underclassmen, but since all transfer students must also take Lib 101, there are also advanced students enrolled.

BACKGROUND

The course was first taught in 1979 when new general education curriculum requirements took effect which sought to provide students with a foundation for their academic careers. It evolved from a variety of one-credit library minicourses given under the aegis of the history department and a 2-week research component of English 101 taught by librarians. As a result of many years of bibliographic instruction by Feinberg librarians and their involvement in the academic governance structure, the college community became convinced of the importance of library research skills and supported their formal inclusion in the curriculum.

Thus, when the general education requirement was revamped in 1978–79, acquiring of basic library skills was made mandatory for all undergraduates, along with writing, communication, and analytical skills. FTE's generated by the course are included in the college total of FTE's.

Initially the course was taught in small class units, but by 1982, the strain on personnel resources necessitated a less demanding format, and large lectures were added with fewer small class meetings. Although adjunct faculty (non-Feinberg librarians) are involved and nonreference librarians also participate, the reference unit, which has primary responsibility for the instruction program, is still considering other options to make the course more manageable in view of limited personnel resources and the pressing needs of other reference services.

COURSE OBJECTIVES

At the end of the course, the student will be able to:
- Relate information problems to types of reference sources and subject areas using an LC class outline and locate these sources in the reference collection.
- Develop approaches for using the author/title catalog and finding diverse Library of Congress terms in the subject catalog.
- Select, locate, and use indexes and abstracting services appropriate to particular information problems.

- Identify and locate periodical titles in the library and determine the format (unbound, bound, microform) of individual issues.
- Identify important bibliographic elements of book and periodical entries for location and evaluation purposes.
- Access and locate materials in the government documents collection.
- Develop a search strategy involving:
  * selection of an appropriate broad subject and use of background sources to formulate a narrow thesis statement for a research paper topic;
  * selection and evaluation, on the basis of relevance and quality, of a periodical article and a monograph related to the research paper topic;
  * identification of important bibliographic elements of book and periodical literature and citation of them according to a given style format.

Course Outline

   I. Organization of library materials; introduction to search strategy
  II. Reference content sources
 III. Book collection: author/title catalog
 IV. Book collection: subject catalog
   V. Indexes and abstracts
 VI. Locating periodicals
VII. Government documents

COURSE REQUIREMENTS

Students are required to attend both lecture and discussion sections, although attendance is not officially taken in the lecture sections. They are given weekly assignments (worksheets) which consist of 25 to 50 multiple-choice questions dealing with specific examples of the tools explained in lecture and discussion sections. These worksheets are graded on a credit/no credit basis, with few points being given for each assignment.

One 3-part assignment, called a "search strategy," requires students to find information on a topic of their choice (they are strongly encouraged to use a topic on which they have been assigned a paper or report for a different class), using an encyclopedia, preferably a subject encyclopedia; a book, specifying which LC subject headings they used and would use to find additional books; and a periodical article, noting which index or abstract was used. Each item selected must be in a correct bibliographic citation. This total assignment accounts for 30 to 40 percent of the grade for the course.

The final exam, a 50-question multiple-choice test, provides 40 to 50 percent of the course grade. Letter grades are given at the end of the course. Starting in spring 1984, it is possible to receive credit for the course by passing a proficiency examination.

No text is required. Turabian's *A Manual for Writers of Term Papers, Theses, and Dissertations* (4th ed., Chicago: University of Chicago Press, 1977), is recommended. It is the standard used for bibliographic citations, and multiple copies are kept available at the reference desk for student use.

Students are able to evaluate the course using a collegewide form. These computer-graded reports enable students to evaluate assignments and lecture quality and content. Results are compiled by the computer center and are not available to instructors until well into the following semester. A departmental evaluation form has also been used.

STRENGTHS AND WEAKNESSES

The course reaches *all* students in the college; that is by far its greatest strength. It puts students in contact with the library and makes the faces of at least a few librarians familiar to them.

One drawback of Lib 101 is that it is given early in a student's college career so that students find it hard to believe that the course will be necessary or applicable for later college work. Aiming it at incoming freshmen also means that its content is limited to a fairly rudimentary level. This bores the more advanced students and limits the challenge to the librarians teaching it.

Because of the large number of students in the course each semester (approximately 700–950), there are many librarians involved in teaching. In addition to 3 to 6 from Feinberg, 3 to 7 adjunct faculty must be hired from the pool of librarians in the area, resulting in some disjointedness and lack of familiarity with the college in general. Administration of a course of this size is extremely difficult for a librarian to manage in addition to the normal duties s/he may have as a reference librarian. A program this large may require the full-time commitment of one librarian to administer it.

The fact that the course is a requirement also has the drawback of relieving many of the rest of the college faculty from involving their students in library research ("they take Library Research Skills, so I don't have to teach them how to do research in my class"). The fact that Lib 101 is a requirement has also resulted in the library's relaxation of recruitment of faculty support. Maybe a reminder to the faculty of the need for assigned papers on which students may then base their search strategies for Lib 101 would help make the course relevant to students, as it would illustrate the continuing relationship between various courses and library research.

A good program of advanced-level courses is necessary to make the basic Library Research Skills course function as just that, a basic course upon which others may build. A long-range plan is to encourage faculty librarians to work with departments in the college to coordinate courses in specific research areas, possibly as a minicourse or as a component of another course. A broader approach such as a course in conducting research in a discipline is another possibility for the future.

COMMENTS

A great improvement in the course was initiated in the spring of 1984 when a Lib 101 information desk was established. Staffed by a part-time adjunct faculty member, the desk is a moveable lectern which is stationed near that part of the library where much of the weekly assignment will be done. The desk is apparently relieving the reference desk of Lib 101 questions while providing direct support to the students while they are working on their assignments. The only further improvement that is needed is more hours of staffing.

The time commitment of librarians to the course is constantly being addressed with varying degrees of success. Some sort of trade-off is necessary in order to allow the librarians teaching to devote as much time as is needed to the course—either a shifting of duties to provide teachers with more time or a system of rotation such as is now in operation may work.

The constant revision of the course is necessary but not to the extent that it has been done in the past. Somewhere, satisfaction with a method must be found so that revision will be limited to materials only and not to the course as a whole. Realistic expectations of students by librarians, and of librarians by themselves, is essential to allow the course to evolve gradually and continually without overwhelming anyone involved in it.

The search strategy assignment currently being used is an attempt to pull together the "tools" aspect of the course so that students may see why those tools are taught. An assignment that clearly shows the student how a good search strategy can produce valuable research, but that also can be graded by librarians without endless hours of checking sources, seems impossible. This is one area in which the number of students becomes a major problem; each instructor has 30 to 120 student assignments to grade in one week, so ease in grading is of paramount importance. How to accomplish this and create an assignment with which the student can understand the research process is a continuing goal of those working on the course.

Case Study #3: Iowa State University

University Library
Ames, Iowa 50011
Gertrude N. Jacobson, Head, Library
Instruction

One of the first land-grant universities, Iowa State is located in the heart of the Midwest. Its 26,000 students are primarily undergraduates, with a large percentage coming from rural areas. There are approximately 1,320,000 volumes in the library's holdings, including 17,500 serials as well as one million microforms. The library faculty is composed of 50 members; library instruction has 4 full-time instructors, a department head, and a secretary.

COURSE DESCRIPTION

Library 160 is a half-credit, half-semester (8 weeks) course required by all colleges of the university. Students receive a grade of satisfactory or fail. The university catalog states that the course must be taken during the freshman year, if possible, or for transfer students, during their first semester at Iowa State. Three thousand students are enrolled per semester in 60 one-hour sessions per week (50 students a section). Four instructors teach these 60 sections. In addition, during fall semester, the head of the department is in charge of 120 honor students in an "as arranged" section, 2 weeks in length.

BACKGROUND

Fanny Thomas, Iowa State librarian, organized a course in library instruction for all members of the freshman class in 1890. The program evolved from a noncredit, nonrequired course to a one-credit, quarter-long, required course in 1973. This course, designed primarily by Matyne Easton, head of library instruction, was a self-help, self-paced plan wherein students could proceed at their own speed.

Prior to changing to the semester system in the fall of 1981, the library instruction staff, assisted by personnel from the media resources center, planned and developed a course using large-screen television. The decision to use this medium was for motivational purposes, to attempt to spark enthusiasm by having students observe their peers going through the procedures they would need to use in learning library usage. Perhaps the largest hurdle was in making the actors believable as role models. Four video-tapes are used in conjunction with lectures and question/answer periods. Each class period is supervised by an instuctor.

COURSE OBJECTIVES

By the end of the course, the student will be able to make the decisions and choices necessary to efficiently do a literature search. This will include proficiency in:

- Locating the various service areas, facilities, and resources available in the ISU library.
- Selecting a subject for this literature search and determining the search strategy to use.
- Obtaining background information from appropriate reference sources.
- Using the *Library of Congress Subject Headings* and the card catalog to obtain monographic information.
- Locating and using appropriate indexing services to obtain references to periodical literature.
- Determining the physical locations of the periodicals and monographs selected.

Course Outline

    I. Introduction to the course, a mini-tour of the library via videotape, and discussion of locations and services
    II. Videotape II: using the card catalog and locating publications
    III. Videotape III: using reference materials and indexing services
    IV. Videotape IV: indexing services assignment
    V. Comprehensive test—first try
    VI. Review
    VII. Comprehensive test—second try

COURSE REQUIREMENTS

The emphasis in the tapes and the course outline is on a literature search, culminating in an indexing services assignment to be handed in at the time of the first test. This assignment is graded by the instructors, using a grading system of satisfactory or unsatisfactory. If the assignment is unsatisfactory, the student must correct it in order to pass the course. Short quizzes may be given during some of the class periods. These are graded but are used only for review purposes. During the indexing services assignment week, instructors are available in the reference area to assist the students if necessary. The examination consists of 64 multiple-choice, matching, and true-false questions; 50 is the passing score.

TEXT

The course manual, prepared by the library instruction staff, is in its 13th edition. In addition to the text material, self-help questions appear at the end of each unit. A laboratory, consisting of a miniature card catalog, indexing services, and reference sources, is available to assist the student in answering these questions. Answers are in the appendix of the manual. The course videotapes, as well as 5 audiotapes which discuss various aspects of the course, are available in the library media center.

EVALUATION

Over the past several years, we have been evaluating the course by collecting statistical information. This information has been used to:

- Analyze difficulty level of test questions.
- Determine the number passing each test.
- Analyze class attendance.
- Determine usage of audiocassettes and videotapes in the media center.
- Analyze reasons for students' failing the course.

Individual instructors have used questionnaires to determine the students' previous experience in libraries, methods used for test preparation, and the length of time spent in studying.

In addition, the course materials have undergone extensive formative evaluation. Whenever the course text is revised, trial versions are reviewed by library and media staff members for accuracy and by students for effectiveness and clarity. During the production of the videotapes, a pilot tape was prepared, shown to students, and evaluated prior to the development of the final draft scripts. The completed tapes were also field-tested and evaluated to confirm their effectiveness.

STRENGTHS AND WEAKNESSES

We feel that the videotapes have definitely proved to be a plus. Class attendance is a primary problem in a required course; however, there now seems to be a greater incentive to come and see what may happen next. The principal problem with the course at the present time stems from the fact that the entire library is being remodelled. It is necessary to update periodically the manual, audiocassettes, and videotapes, which is costly. In 2 years, however, this situation should stabilize.

Case Study #4: University of California–Berkeley

The School of Library and Information Studies in conjunction with the General Library
Berkeley, California 94720
Patricia S. Vanderberg, Associate Librarian II, Bancroft Library

The University of California–Berkeley is the original campus of the 9-campus university system. The majority of the 30,000 students at Berkeley are Californians, but many students come from every part of the United States and 100 foreign countries to study in nearly 300 degree programs. One quarter of the student population consists of minorities. Admission to the university is very competitive.

The university library system consists of 3 major libraries, 23 branch libraries, and numerous special libraries. Their combined holdings total more than 6 million volumes, 100,000 current serial publications, 44 million manuscripts, 2 million microforms, 300,000 maps, and 40,000 sound recordings. Many of the 125 librarians participate in some kind of instructional activity, and 8 are regular instructors of Bibliography I.

COURSE DESCRIPTION

Bibliography I: Methods of Library Use is a formal 3-credit course offered by the School of Library and Information Studies. The course is an elective for undergraduates and consists of 3 hours of class per week for a full semester. Usually one-third of each class period is spent in the classroom and the other two-thirds is spent working on assignments at one of the campus libraries, although the course organization varies with each instructor. The basic instructional format is also generously supplemented by library tours, online database demonstrations, media presentations, and individual conferences. Seventeen or 18 sections of this course are offered each semester and are all taught by librarians.

BACKGROUND

Bibliography I began as an experimental 2-credit course in the fall of 1968. Seven sections of the course were taught by staff members of the general library, who were allotted one-quarter released time from their regular assignments. It was based on no previous model and grew out of a proposal written by librarian Charles H. Shain in 1965. Professor Ray E. Held was also instrumental in designing the academic framework for the course and lending it administrative and financial support from the School of Librarianship. There were some initial difficulties in establishing a stable source of funding, but these difficulties ended in 1971 when the library school assumed full administrative responsibility for the course.

In the early 1970s, the course was expanded from 2 to 4 units with sessions meeting twice weekly for 90 minutes. At that time, instructors began to be appointed for one-third rather than one-quarter time. The library school also began to recruit general instructors (whose salaries are entirely paid by the school) in addition to regular staff members of the general library in order to meet the ever-increasing demand for more sections of the course.

MARKETING

Posters in the campus libraries as well as sign-up sheets at the reference desks were the first ways in which students were informed of the existence of Bibliography I. Enrollment in the course particularly increased in response to a course critique that appeared in a student review of courses on the Berkeley campus. In recent years, the course has been advertised in a variety of ways, such as through ads in campus newspapers, fliers, posters, bulletin board announcements, class visits, letters to faculty and students, and publicity on library tours and at orientation programs. Another incentive for undergraduates to take this course is that they receive a main library stack pass while they are enrolled in the course and a permanent stack pass if they earn an "A" in the course.

COURSE OBJECTIVES

By the end of the course, students should:

- Gain a working familiarity with library resources available at UC/Berkeley, which has more than 60 libraries and over 6 million volumes.
- Learn to develop a systematic method of research which can then be applied to the writing of future term papers, reports, and theses.
- Become skilled in research techniques that will enable them to use any library more effectively.

Course Outline

1. Introduction to the library system and tour of the main library
2. Card, microfiche, and online catalogs
3. Catalog records, forms of entry, and filing rules
4. Subject catalogs, classification, and keyword indexes
5. Checking out library materials, national and trade bibliographies, and interlibrary borrowing
6. Introduction to research strategies: topic selection and effective note-taking
7. Introduction to reference materials: reference guides, bibliographies, encyclopedias, and compendia
8. Dictionaries, directories, and biographical sources
9. Geographical sources: maps, atlases, gazeteers, and travel guides
10. Periodicals: abstracts, indexes, catalogs, and citation indexes
11. Newspapers and microforms: abstracts, indexes, and catalogs

12. Nonperiodical indexes: dissertations and theses; literary indexes; book, play, and movie reviews
13. Government documents and statistical sources
14. Computer-assisted literature searching
15. Audiovisual media sources
16. Planning a term project: comprehensive research strategy, guides to evaluation, and bibliographic citations
17. UC/Berkeley libraries and beyond: how to approach "new" libraries
18. Tours of various libraries: map room, government documents, the Bancroft Library, Pacific Film Archive, Berkeley Public Library, etc.
19. Completion of a substantial annotated bibliography with a discussion of the research strategy for a topic of the student's choice

COURSE REQUIREMENTS

Bibliography I class sessions consist of lectures to explain new material and review old assignments, library tours, computer demonstrations, individual conferences to discuss the term project, and in-class and take-home assignments which are designed to give students practical experience in using the UC/Berkeley libraries. Assignments may be either specific problem sets to utilize particular library resources such as the catalogs or they may be tailored to each student's work on the term project. The term project is a carefully annotated bibliography of 25 to 30 citations, on a topic of the student's choice, which demonstrates knowledge and effective utilization of library resources. It includes an introduction, a discussion of search strategies, and the criteria the student has used to compile the annotations.

The annotated bibliography portion of the term project consists of 3 parts: an accurate and consistent bibliographic citation; source and location of the item; and a summary, evaluation, and recommendation for inclusion of the item in the bibliography. This selective bibliography may be done in conjunction with a research paper students are required to write for another course. Essentially, the term project constitutes 50 percent of the grade, weekly assignments are 20 percent, quizzes are 20 percent, and class participation and attendance are 10 percent of the grade.

The only text for the course is *Methods of Library Use: Handbook for Bibliography I,* edited by Signe Peterson and Marta Fuchs Winkik (Berkeley, CA: School of Library and Information Studies, University of California/Berkeley, July 1982, reprinted with minor revisions July 1983). Some instructors supplement this text with library orientation leaflets or other texts such as *Guide to the Use of Libraries and Information Sources,* by Jean Key Gates (New York: McGraw-Hill, 1983).

At the end of each semester, students are asked to complete an evaluation form. They rate the value of the course content, the amount of work required, the instructor, and the worth of assignments and course activities. They also comment on the services and librarians at the various campus libraries, and these comments are shared with the appropriate members of those libraries mentioned.

STRENGTHS AND WEAKNESSES

The strengths of Bibliography I are that it is a well-established general academic course and the instruction is not standardized but tailored to the specific needs of both the instructor and the students. However, these very strengths sometimes also prove to be weaknesses. For example, many librarians have taught Bibliography I, and each has brought something different and unique to the course; however, few librarians remain instructors long enough to foster a sense of continuity and to make systematic improvements in the course.

The fact that the course is so broad-based in its appeal results in classes being full of people with diverse interests and at quite different levels of bibliographic sophistication. In these instances, it is difficult for the instructor to gauge the appropriate level of instruction and sustain everyone's interest. On the whole, though, Bibliography I has been remarkably successful in that it has provided from 500 to 800 undergraduates annually with a thorough orientation to the UC/Berkeley library system and resources. The research methods and skills acquired by students in the course should prove useful throughout their lives.

Case Study #5: The Evergreen State College

Daniel J. Evans Library
Olympia, Washington 98505
Mary M. Huston, Faculty Research
Librarian

The Evergreen State College (TESC) is a state-supported, liberal arts college founded in the late 60s. The 44 staff members and 190,000 volumes in the library support the research needs of 2,700 undergraduates, 80 graduates, and 134 faculty. The basic educational philosophy of the college involves a multidisciplinary, multicultural approach. Learning revolves around small seminars in which participants discuss readings for the week and make connections between that and lectures, labs, and workshops. Because individual and small group research projects are frequently required of students, library usage is high.

TEACHING STRATEGIES

Education at the college is intended to enable students to think for themselves, to be able to find, analyze, and interpret information independently in preparation for capably participating in the decision making affecting their lives both in and out of school. To facilitate this, we librarians offering information instruction at Evergreen have had to reassess traditional educational philosophies and practices. For example, we have largely repositioned ourselves in the classroom. Rather than assuming the conventional roles of experts and initiates, librarians and students work together as resource persons, learning together to make sense of research experience.

To codiscover information patterns and principles has required that we not operate initially from a straight bibliographic point of departure. The creation of information, for instance, is presented first to students as a cultural phenomenon. Using such an approach, information is considered—not in terms of bibliographic organization—but rather in terms of the sectors of society and human enterprise from which information about different subjects, packaged in different formats, arises. Following this classroom discussion, we introduce the publication cycle as a model for understanding how some knowledge is produced, thereby connecting students' experiential knowledge with librarians' bibliographic knowledge.

This teaching strategy largely removes the librarians from the position of expert: our pedagogical stance becomes that of a facilitator who encourages students to draw from their own experiences with social organization. Our role becomes more like that of a journalist than that of a librarian; that is, we would ask questions (who, what, when, where, why) and discover information *with* the students. And, significantly, it recognizes and extends students' strengths rather than ours.

Beginning instruction with what students know and then bridging the gap between students' and librarians' knowledge is also the basis for the problem-solving workshops in the research course. One such workshop used a short story, "A Jury of Her Peers" by Susan Keating Glaspell, as a vehicle for cultivating in students the recognition that a detective's investigation for clues is analogous to a researcher's search for evidence, and, by implication, that students could transfer what they knew from other information-seeking experiences to library research. In that exercise, students worked in small groups to analyze the questions and processes that the detectives and the defendant's friends used in their respective investigations.

As a bridge to the bibliographic environment, students next had to analyze the respective characters' investigations in terms of Marcia Bates's idea tactics. They then had to combine the most successful of the characters' strategies in a letter to the defendant's lawyer advising her on a literature search to support her case. The letter had to provide specific search questions and discuss the parameters of the information required. The following week, students had to draw upon what they had learned in the workshop to reformulate their own research questions for the quarter and to develop a tentative literature searching strategy.

By design, the workshops require that students work independently of the librarian instructors and "discover" (frequently in small groups) their own answers to problems. These carefully constructed exercises build students' confidence in their ability to make research decisions collaboratively, and that confidence carries over into students' individual work. It also establishes a pattern of students recognizing and using each others' strengths.

Equalizing student and librarian status in the classroom is furthered by our expectation that students will become experts on their topic during the quarter. Although students frequently consult with us throughout the course on their research, they rapidly acquire more expertise on their topic than we have, so we naturally begin to speak to each other as coexperts. As the quarter progresses, this lessening of boundaries becomes obvious, too, in the research observation sessions which begin each class period. Largely in lieu of lectures (and in the spirit of a graduate school seminar), students and librarians work together in these sessions to make sense of students' research experience. Our ability to talk comfortably as a group is furthered by the small group work in the workshops and by the largely conversational style which occurs because 2 librarians team-teach the course. We've found all of these strategies—reducing the hierarchical nature of the classroom, basing explanations and exercises on student experiences, encouraging collaborative student work, and expecting student expertise—to be important contributions to the development of students' confidence and skills, important prerequisites for personal empowerment.

COURSE DESCRIPTION

The Library Research Methodology course is offered 4 hours a week during each of the 3 quarters of the regular academic year. Generally, 2 credits are granted for (theoretical) information studies and 2 credits are granted for (applied) research methodology. The conceptual foundations and accompanying skills for library research are presented during the first weeks of the course. Topics include library classification and access systems, the structure of disciplinary literatures, the publication cycle and primary and secondary sources, research question (and subquestion) formulation, and locational and factual reference tools.

Building on this foundation, students spend the remaining two-thirds of the quarter developing a multidisciplinary bibliography of about 80 citations. In addition to monographic and periodical material in each of the 3 disciplines of social sciences, arts and humanities, and pure and applied science, each bibliography must include federal government documents, alternative press publications, and nonprint resources. Students assess their citations in the final weeks of the quarter; this evaluation requires clarification of the parameters of their bibliographies, including consideration of such issues as the ideological points of view to be represented.

During the quarter, then, students become informed on 2 levels—a topical level and a bibliographic level. They learn about their subjects through writing annotations for selected information sources in their bibliographies and enhance their research expertise by applying increasingly sophisticated research techniques in their searching. Their investigations are detailed in a research journal.

LEARNING OUTCOMES

The course is intended to introduce students to library research methods and concepts so that they can function effectively in modern libraries and information centers, using a variety of information sources, including print, nonprint, and machine-readable resources. More specifically, students are expected to understand the organization of Evergreen's library and its major research tools and be able to transfer this knowledge to other information centers and access tools.

Secondly, students are informed of the existence of highly organized information systems and of the wide variety of available access tools and information resources; they are expected to develop competency in the selection and use of information. Ultimately, the aim of the course is to develop informed library users who, independently, can locate and assess sources of information.

Although there are no academic prerequisites, students are required to have a topic of interest identified before they can register for the course. This requirement and establishing a class size limit of 15 (with 2 librarian instructors), has ensured us of a cohesive, motivated group of student researchers.

Each student receives a narrative evaluation of his/her work at the end of the quarter. Evaluation is based on a student's own progress during the quarter; s/he is not compared to other students. In turn, each student writes a course evaluation, librarian instructor evaluations, and a self-evaluation. The course revisions made each quarter rely heavily on the content of student evaluations of the course. Currently, we are working on better integrating nonprint into the course and on strengthening the course work on information evaluation.

Kate Turabian's *Manual for the Writing of Term Papers, Theses, and Dissertations* (4th ed., Chicago, University of Chicago Press, 1977) is the official style manual for the course. In addition, students are required to purchase the course "text," a collection of locally developed bibliographic instruction materials.

BACKGROUND

A credit-generating library research course has been offered at TESC since 1974. In the early years of the course, librarians introduced students to key research tools in each of 10 academic fields. Students developed a research question and bibliography in each field. In 1980, the first syllabus incorporating problem-solving strategies and conceptual research models was developed. For 3 years, significant revisions have been made from quarter to quarter, in an attempt to better blend bibliographic theory and application.

Librarian authors who have influenced the course content include Elizabeth Frick, Ray McInnis, Cerise Oberman, Mary Reichel, Pamela Kobelski, and Donna Rubens. TESC librarians who have taught the course one or more times and thereby have influenced its direction are Kelley Emmons, Mary Huston, Pat Matheny-White, Debbie Robinson, and Susan Perry. Additionally, several TESC librarians have taught specific sessions of the course: Lucy Enriquez, Raúl Huerta, Frank Motley, Sarah Pedersen, and Malcolm Stilson.

REFERENCES

Bates, M.J. (1979). Idea tactics (to help generate new ideas or solutions to problems in information searching). *Journal of the American Society for Information Science, 30,* 280–289.

Glasspell, S.G. (1983). A jury of her peers. In Lee R. Edwards and Arlyn Diamond (Eds.), *American voices, American women.* New York: Avon.

FOR FURTHER READING

Bates, M.J. (1979). Information search tactics. *Journal of the American Society for Information Science, 30,* 205–214.

Finkel, D.L., and Monk, G.S. (1983). Teachers and learning groups: Dissolution of the Atlas complex. In C. Boutin and R. Gaith (Eds.), *Learning in groups* (pp. 83–97). San Francisco, CA: Jossey-Bass.

Frick, E. (1975). Information structure and bibliographic instruction. *Journal of Academic Librarianship, 1,* 12–14.

Huston, M.M. (1981). Dialogue and debate: Rethinking our approach to research instruction. *Research Strategies 1,* 185–186.

Kobelski, P., and Reichel, M. (1981). Conceptual frameworks for bibliographic instruction. *Journal of Academic Librarianship, 7,* 73–77.

Motley, F., and Huston, M. (1981). Faculty membership for librarians: The Evergreen State College model. In *Options for the 80's.* Papers presented at the Association of College and Research Libraries, Second National Conference, Minneapolis, Minnesota, October 1–4, 1981.

Oberman, C., and Linton, R.A. (1982). Guided design: Teaching library research as problem-solving. In C. Oberman and K. Strauch (Eds.), *Theories of bibliographic instruction: Designs for teaching* (pp. 111–134). New York: Bowker.

Case Study #6: Miami University

Department of Educational Media
Oxford, Ohio 45056
Jack E. Daugherty
Associate Professor and Coordinator, EDM 251

Miami University is one of 12 4-year publicly supported universities in Ohio. Of the 14,870 students enrolled, 13,423 are undergraduates enrolled in one of the 6 undergraduate divisions of the university. Admission is competitive.

The library contains over a million volumes, a million microforms, and 5,000 periodicals and newspapers. In addition to thousands of recordings and other nonprint materials, there is a map collection of 80,000.

COURSE DESCRIPTION

EDM 251: Effective Use of Libraries is a 2-credit-hour course offered each of two semesters with, historically, 17 sections in the first semester and 14 sections in the second semester. Sections are limited to 30 students. Typically, there are majors from all divisions and of all class standings (freshmen through seniors), with primary enrollment from the School of Business. Fall enrollment is ordinarily in the vicinity of 500, with spring's at 400.

All lectures are delivered in a classroom outside (but adjacent to) the library, and follow-through lab sessions are conducted in part in the university library and/or the classroom. Most lab sessions are based upon the completion of a worksheet related to the lecture. For the most part, student assignments are individualized. For one unit, there might be 30 individualized worksheets, with no 2 students completing the same problems. (Design of these is extremely time-consuming when initially done.) The class meets one session each week for a period of 110 minutes.

Six instructors presently teach the course. Three are full-time members of the educational media department, while the other 3 teach part-time as needed. None are on the university library staff. The coordinator is responsible for preparing all materials. His lectures are monitored by the other instructors to ensure course continuity as well as to provide for feedback.

BACKGROUND

The course was first offered on a trial basis in the fall of 1977 with an enrollment of 22. It was modeled on experiences gleaned during the course of teaching basic reference courses for many years and through reference work in many different library settings. Assistance from others teaching the course has been in the form of developing individual student problems for assignments. Readjustment and change of subject matter is ongoing and has primarily taken the form of reducing the number of sources discussed, with a greater shift of emphasis to strategy, problem solving, and critical thinking.

MARKETING

A 1983 study to determine why students were enrolling in the course revealed peer recommendations—word-of-mouth—to be the single most important factor. Given the fact that the course is not required by any university department, promotional techniques are ongoing and intense. Some divisions list the course as a suggested elective for incoming freshmen, and it is listed and described in a publication distributed to all incoming freshmen. Additionally, flyers are posted at key points at various "change of program" periods throughout the year. The latter has brought in significant enrollment at the critical time when students are often seeking additional courses to complete their schedules. The fact that the course is for 2 credit hours is appealing.

COURSE OBJECTIVES

The course aims to:

- Develop the learner's self-confidence in the ability to successfully utilize libraries and library resources.
- Develop the learner's ability to employ effective strategies for solving information needs.
- Familiarize learners with the basic reference sources of a general nature.
- Familiarize learners with basic reference sources of their chosen discipline.
- Familiarize learners with the basic organization of, and services offered, by libraries.

Course Outline

1. Orientation/library tour
2. Retrieving materials
3. Card catalog
4. *Library of Congress Subject Headings List*
5. Periodical indexes and abstracting services
6. *Essay and General Literature Index*
7. Newspaper and current events sources
8. Indexes to book reviews
9. Bibliography
10. Biographical sources; tracings on catalog cards
11. Encyclopedias, yearbook, and handbooks
12. Micromaterials and other nonprint resources
13. Automated retrieval systems
14. Government documents
15. Search strategy included in most lectures

COURSE REQUIREMENTS

Completion of 10 worksheets is required, and these constitute 50 percent of the final grade. Each deals with a specific subject, such as card catalog, use of subject periodical indexes, etc. In addition, there are 5 homework assignments. Some instructors administer quizzes, while others require the completion of a bibliography. There are midterm and final examinations, which are primarily multiple-choice and computer-scored, and which constitute 35 percent of the final grade. All of the foregoing, along with other variables such as penalty points for work submitted late, are included in calculating the final grade.

No commercially published text is used. The course coordinator has written several readings dealing with the course materials. These readings are distributed to students.

A universitywide evaluation form is administered at the end of the course, and great care is taken to ensure confidentiality. No instructor is permitted to administer this to his/her students, and instructors do not have access to evaluations until final grades have been submitted. Half of the evaluation form is comprised of questions for which responses are on a scale of one to 4, while the remaining are provided for written comments, which are encouraged.

STRENGTHS AND WEAKNESSES

The major weakness of the course is that it is not linked to informational needs and actual assignments in other classes. (However, students are encouraged to share any such library-oriented assignments, and this often triggers brainstorming sessions from which all profit.) To counteract this weakness, informational needs of former enrollees are discussed to illustrate the relevance of the subject matter of the lecture. Numerous such previous student inquiries are interspersed throughout the lecture notes of each and every session.

Given the individualized nature of the worksheets, grading is time-consuming. Maintenance of lab copies of indexes and such requires the considerable attention of student assistants. To counteract permanent defacing of indexes, students are required to use pencils, allowing for erasure. (Since students historically mark their textbooks with felt-tip pens and have that procedure ingrained in their minds, it is absolutely futile to aspire to the notion that they will not check, underline, or circle index pages.)

A master file is maintained of the page and column where each answer can be found. After any one given unit is completed, all indexes are checked and erased appropriately. This is done so that students will be required to search pages for appropriate answers rather than find them conveniently identified by another student. It is suggested that permanent runs of indexes not be used, even though more desirable and closer to reality, in order to avoid permanent defacing.

A coordinator is necessary for overseeing all ingredients of a course offered on the scale of EDM 251. These ingredients include preparation of all lecture notes, audiovisual materials, worksheets, assignments, examinations, as well as index maintenance, public relations endeavors, and communication with the library staff.

The course has been most favorably received by students. Previous enrollees are frequently encountered on campus and they pass on high words of praise to all teaching the course. Most students feel the course should be required.

If nothing else is achieved, the course creates student awareness of the wealth of available library resources; that there is more, perhaps, to the effective use of the card catalog or periodical indexes than previously thought; and that one should seek the assistance of librarians. Whereas at the outset, most students admit the size of the university library is intimidating, the majority exit with an air of confidence that they can find what they want independently or with the help of a librarian.

Finally, a valuable fringe benefit of the course—even though not consciously intended when it was conceptualized—is that it tends to sharpen the listening, reading, and transcribing skills of students as they pursue assignments.

Case Study #7: Miami University

Science Library
Oxford, Ohio 45056
Nancy Moeckel, Science Librarian

EDM 252: Scientific Information Sources is a 2-hour, semester-long course intended for science majors in their sophomore year; nonscience majors and upperclassmen do enroll as well. The class meets twice a week for one hour with all homework assignments done outside of class. EDM 252 has been offered both in the fall and spring semesters, but in the future will be offered only in the fall.

BACKGROUND

The course was conceived by 2 science librarians, David Tyckoson (who has since left Miami) and Nancy Moeckel. The educational media department was already offering a very popular class (see Case Study #6), which teaches basic skills using mainly social science and humanities sources for examples. We felt that EDM 252 would provide science majors with necessary in-depth research skills and experiences, using only science materials for exercises. Many science teaching faculty expressed delight in such a course, but since we were offering it to all science majors, we did not want to attach it to one particular department and thereby turn away or frighten any prospective students. Cross-numbering the course over 10 departments was not practical, and the EDM department was more than willing to sponsor our proposal.

Completing the necessary paperwork was perhaps the most difficult hurdle encountered. A course may be taught experimentally, one time only, with only the department chair and dean's approval required. This we had without hesitation, and the class was offered in the fall 1982 semester.

However, by the time it passed official channels to become a permanent offering, it was late summer of 1983 and the deadline for inclusion in printed schedules was long past. No one knew the course existed and most returning students completed their schedules in April, before going home for the summer. Fall 1983 enrollment was not sufficient and the course was not taught. However, spring 1984 enrollment was significant and EDM 252 was offered.

MARKETING

The EDM department announces 252 in all of its sections of 251 and advertises all of its classes at delayed registration. Flyers are posted on all of the science department bulletin boards, and science faculty are asked to announce the course, both in class and to their advisees. Many do so. Flyers are also posted throughout the library and at the circulation and reference desks.

COURSE OBJECTIVES

The course aims to:

- Provide students with the skills necessary to conduct effective and efficient library research.
- Provide students with a basic understanding of the nature of scientific literature and how it differs from other literatures.
- Familiarize students with the major science indexes and abstracts (especially *Biological Abstracts, Chemical Abstracts,* and *Science Citation Index.*
- Provide each student with a basic knowledge of library resources and research techniques in the science discipline of his/her major.

Course Outline

The general content is as listed below, but minor areas can be expanded or contracted depending on the class majors and experiences.
1. Introduction to scientific literature; how scientists communicate
2. General science reference sources (including government documents)
3. Physical sciences; general sources
4. Chemistry
5. Physics/geology
6. Math/computer sciences
7. Engineering/applied science/other specialized areas
8. Life sciences; general sources
9. Botany
10. Zoology
11. Medicine/microbiology
12. Environmental sciences
13. Citation indexing
14. Online searching, special collections, special topics.

COURSE REQUIREMENTS

All class time is used in discussion and/or demonstration of selected tools. Approximately 15 homework assignments are given, all to be completed outside of class. Assignments dealing with major tools or concepts are worth more points. Originally 2 tests were scheduled, but now 3 are. Students appreciate having less material to study for on each test.

The final exam is a take-home test. Each student must compile a bibliography on a subject of his/her choice, following specific guidelines (e.g., using 2 sources from the 3 major indexes/abstracts, 2 from an index of choice, only 3 books). Therefore the final is a practical application of the semester's study.

Homework, the 3 tests, and the final each count as one-third of the final grade. No text is required. Homework assignments require the students to use the tools under discussion. Selected reserve readings are made available, but few students have used them as they are not currently required reading but are intended as self-help readings.

Students complete a standardized, universitywide evaluation form which has ample room for comments. Students have offered constructive criticism, both on these forms and throughout the class. We also ask for comments at midterm on a form of our own devising. In this way, we can incorporate suggestions before the semester is over. This has been helpful, both in teaching and for the students.

STRENGTHS AND WEAKNESSES

The intent of the course is to expose science majors to a wide variety of tools, not just those that are available in their own narrow disciplines. We stress that most disciplines can make use of *Chemical Abstracts,* for example, and we prove this to the geology, botany, and microbiology students, as well as the chemistry majors. Teaching students to broaden their perspectives on what is available in a library is a major strength of this class.

The inherent danger or weakness in any class such as this is the tendency to overinstruct, to create librarians instead of simply competent, confident library users who know their limitations and are not afraid to ask for help. Homework assignments and test questions have to be carefully constructed, to measure search skills and understanding at the user level, not the librarian level.

Case Study #8: State University of New York College of Environmental Science and Forestry

Moon Library
Syracuse, New York 13210
Elizabeth A. Elkins, Associate Librarian and Coordinator of Public Services

SUNY College of Environmental Science and Forestry (ESF) is one of 3 specialized colleges within the SUNY system. Since 1980, the college has been a totally upper-division and graduate school. Approximately 940 undergraduate and 430 graduate students study in the areas of resource management, engineering, environment design, and the physical and life sciences. The library has around 80,000 volumes and currently receives over 800 periodical titles; ESF students also have full access to all library facilities at Syracuse University. Of the 7 library faculty, the 3 public services librarians teach Library 300.

COURSE DESCRIPTION

Library Research Methods, Library 300, is a one-credit course taught during one segment of the semester with 3 hours of class each week (for a total of 15 hours). A typical semester will have 6 sections of 20 students each. FTE's generated by the course are credited to the library. (Librarians have faculty status and the library functions as a separate department.)

Usually the course is offered during the first 5 weeks of the semester, but some sections are delayed to allow the students to become familiar with the research projects in their other courses so that Library 300 will be more meaningful. Classes are kept at 20 students each and are conducted in a small classroom within the library. Each session contains a lecture and/or demonstration of some portion of the search strategy. Often, time is allowed for work sessions so that students can apply immediately what has just been explained.

BACKGROUND

Library 300 was developed as a result of course-related lectures. A number of faculty members who had routinely invited librarians into their classrooms suggested that a separate course be developed for credit. In the fall of 1973, the library faculty submitted a course proposal to the campus curriculum committee, which initially rejected it. This committee felt the format looked restrictive and was concerned that a library course—a skills course—was inappropriate for library credit. Consequently, the library offered a noncredit minicourse in the spring of 1974 as a trial balloon before submitting a revised course proposal based on the success of this experiment.

A credit course was subsequently approved and has been taught each semester since the fall 1974 semester. The scenario of how the course was approved was fully described by Jacquelyn Morris in her paper, "Gaining Faculty Acceptance and Support of Library Instruction: A Case Study," delivered at the 5th Annual Conference on Library Orientation and Instruction at Eastern Michigan University, Ypsilanti, Michigan, May 1975.

Library 300 could be described as a course-related credit course. It is usually taken in conjunction with another course on campus which requires a major research paper. Today Library 300 is built into 5 specific curricula, usually at the junior level: biology, chemistry, paper science and engineering, landscape architecture, and environmental studies.

MARKETING

Over the years, information about Library 300 has spread primarily by word-of-mouth. The course is listed in the college catalog and is offered each semester. The library reminds patrons of the availability of the course through library information handouts and a library newsletter.

COURSE OBJECTIVES

The goal of Library 300 has remained the same since its inception: to develop the students' ability to identify, locate, and process information. Specifically, the students will, upon completion of the course, be able to:

- Plan and implement an efficient search strategy using library, campus, and other information systems as appropriate.
- Locate, evaluate, and select appropriate materials. Each student compiles a subject bibliography on a topic which can then be used for another course.

The needs and topics of the students enrolled in Library 300 are different. The course, therefore, was designed with flexibility to accommodate these different needs. An attempt is made to keep the class sections homogeneous (i.e., chemistry students enroll in one section, biology students in another). Regardless of the students' topics, they need a strategy or plan for searching their literature.

Course Outline

The following course outline represents the strategy taught to the students:

1. Introduction—understanding resource literature and the need for a search strategy
2. Library Basics—learning about the library to be used, what is available and where (basic orientation)
3. Topic Selection—selecting and clearly defining a topic, including the use of literature reviews and other background sources

4. Subject Catalogs—searching the subject catalog for monographs including a thorough understanding of Library of Congress subject headings, and retrieving the material identified
5. Extending the Search for Books—using other sources (i.e., surrogate catalogs such as book or online catalogs for other collections as well as *Books in Print* and *Cumulative Book Index*)
6. Indexes and Abstracts—identifying appropriate periodical indexes and abstracts, learning to use them, and searching them for the present topic in hand
7. Locating Serials—retrieving original periodical sources identified through the index and abstract search, including the use of union lists and interlibrary loan as appropriate
8. Alternative Sources—exploring alternative sources and methods of retrieving material, e.g., computer searches, interviews, government documents, and reference books
9. The Bibliography—evaluating all sources located and compiling a bibliography and a scope note which defines the topic and explains how the bibliography is arranged and why

This search strategy is documented in *Library Searching: Resources and Strategies with Examples from the Environmental Sciences* (New York: Jeffrey Norton, 1978), written by Jacquelyn M. Morris and Elizabeth A. Elkins. The text was developed from the handout material used in the first years of Library 300. *Library Searching,* while out-of-date to some extent and also out of print, is still required reading for students because the basic strategy outlined by the text works.

COURSE REQUIREMENTS

The students complete a series of exercises which log their search process. Each exercise is assigned a number of points which total 100. The final exercise is the compilation of the subject bibliography and is worth 20 of the 100 total points. There are no tests or final exams. The workbook which contains these exercises is revised each year and includes input from the current instructors of the course.

Library 300 students are given the opportunity to evaluate the course upon its completion through a one-page list of questions about the course, its content, and method of instruction. These student concerns are often incorporated in workbook and course revisions.

The focus of Library 300 is not on the use of specific sources but on a search strategy or process which may be transferred and applied to other learning situations. Sources come and go and topics change, but the process will remain. Library 300 not only helps students in a very practical way with a specific and current research project but, hopefully, helps the students develop skills which will enable them to be productive lifelong learners.

Case Study #9: State University of New York at Oswego

Penfield Library
Oswego, New York 13126
Mignon S. Adams, Coordinator of
Information Services

SUNY/Oswego is one of SUNY's 13 arts and sciences colleges. Its 7,500 students, mostly undergraduates, come primarily from within the state. Admission is competitive. The library holds over 300,000 volumes and receives about 2,000 periodicals. Twelve of the 17 librarians are involved in library instruction.

COURSE DESCRIPTION

General Studies 100H: Introduction to Library Research is a one-hour course, taught once a year as an elective for freshmen and sophomores admitted to a special honors program. Other students may take it with the permission of the instructor. The course lasts for half a semester, beginning 2 weeks after the semester starts, and consists of 7 weekly 2-hour sessions. Typically, half of each period is spent in the classroom and the other half in the library working on assignments.

BACKGROUND

The course was first taught in 1979 in the first year of Oswego's honor program. It was modeled after the 2-hour course taught at Oswego since 1975 which was, in turn, modeled after a course taught at the SUNY College of Environmental Science and Forestry (see previous case study). The earlier course, first taught by Blanche Judd, head of reference, had initially been taught under the aegis of the English department; after 2 successful years, the college curriculum committee was willing to consider it as one of 3 general studies courses. Due to the success of the previous course and the interest of the director of the honors program (a friend as well as a colleague), the honors course had no problems being accepted.

Advisement for honors students is done by the honors director, who has consistently recommended the course. Most of the students have been concurrently taking a course in intellectual history for which they write a paper, and the librarian has worked closely with the history professor in suggesting appropriate topics and citation style.

COURSE OBJECTIVES

At the end of the course, students will be able to:

- Choose an appropriate broad subject and narrow it to a manageable topic for a research paper.
- Find suitable and diverse subject headings in the card catalog.
- Locate and use special indexes appropriate to a major area of interest.
- Evaluate monographic and periodical literature as to its credibility, usefulness, and level of scholarship.
- Identify important bibliographic elements and arrange them according to a given style sheet.
- Identify types of reference works appropriate for information needs.

Course Outline

    I. Introduction to the library; writing correct bibliographic citations
    II. Deciding upon a researchable topic; locating background information
    III. Using the subject card catalog
    IV. Locating, using, and evaluating periodical literature
    V. Using various reference and statistical sources; locating and using book reviews
    VI. Locating information in one's own major

COURSE REQUIREMENTS

Students are encouraged to take the course at the same time they're taking another course which requires a research paper or project, and most do. There are 5 fairly lengthy exercises, based on the units of the course, which students complete using the topic of their choice. For example, the periodicals assignment asks them to locate an article on their topic in a general index, a special index, and an abstracting service; to compare these 3 types of tools; to compare an article for a general magazine with one from a scholarly journal; and to fill out an interlibrary loan form. A final project is required, which consists of a scope note and bibliography cards for their research papers. There is a brief quiz over assigned readings and a final examination which covers the objectives of the course. Grades (A–E) are assigned on the basis of student work.

No text is required, but a copy of *Researching and Writing in History,* by F. N. McCoy (Berkeley, CA: University of California Press, 1974), is placed on reserve and a quiz covering several chapters is given. Students researching a nonhistory topic may choose to read and be tested on several chapters from *Library Searching: Resources and Strategies with Examples from the Environmental Sciences,* by Jacquelyn M. Morris and Elizabeth A. Elkins (New York: Jeffrey Norton, 1978), or *A Short Guide to Independent Study and Research in Literature,* by Bryan Gillespie (Deland, FL: Everett/Edwards, 1975). Students are encouraged to purchase a copy of either the MLA or the APA style manual, but only a few do.

Students complete an evaluation form at the end of each course. They respond to the value of each assignment as well as to the value of the course as a whole, rate the instructor, and make suggestions for future classes.

STRENGTHS AND WEAKNESSES

The honors library course reaches only a small number of students; only 25 honors students are admitted to Oswego each year, and honors classes are restricted to 15 participants. However, since the course is fairly standardized, the amount of time required for the librarian teaching it is not excessive.

The course was taught in the spring semester during its first 2 years of existence. It was changed to the fall semester at the request of other honors faculty, who felt students should acquire library skills at the beginning of their college careers. However, the class was less successful: first semester students (who had all been excellent high school students) did not sense a need to learn about the library, as compared to those who had already attempted researching a long paper in a college library. The course is now being changed back to spring semester.

Another problem has been the scope of the final project, which students complained was time-consuming, and which we also found enormously laborious to grade. The project is now being revamped.

Case Study #10: Pennsylvania State University

University Libraries
University Park, Pennsylvania 16802
Mary Ellen Larson, Senior Assistant
Librarian

The Pennsylvania State University is the land-grant university of the Commonwealth of Pennsylvania. Over 60,000 students pursue degrees—the majority of undergraduates reside in Pennsylvania and its contiguous states, while graduate students attend the university from all over the world (many from Third World countries). Admission is competitive.

The University Libraries contain over 2 million cataloged volumes, a million documents, 23,500 periodicals, 253,000 maps, 55,000 pictures, approximately 2 million microfilms, and over 2 million other bibliographical items. The library has developed LIAS, its integrated online catalog. Of the 90 librarians, a number participate in the credit and noncredit bibliographic instruction program.

Under the direction of Elizabeth G. Ellis, head of library studies, 7 service courses are offered, including a basic survey course, and others in bibliographic information resources and systems, archival management, federal government publications and legal resources, and business information resources. In addition, 7 common course numbers (e.g., special topics, independent study, etc.) allow the tailoring of a course to student information needs and enrollment numbers.

COURSE DESCRIPTION

Library Studies 301H: Information Research Methods and Systems is a one-credit course, taught once a year as an elective primarily for juniors in the University Scholars program and the College of Liberal Arts honors program. Other students may enroll with permission of the instructor. The course meets once a week for 15 weeks and is taught using a lecture-discussion method. The final 3 class periods are devoted to the presentation of a bibliographic research project.

BACKGROUND

The course was first offered in the fall semester of 1983. It was originally offered in conjunction with the honors program in the College of Liberal Arts and then attracted the attention of the University Scholars Program, which draws its students from all schools and disciplines. During their junior or senior years, both groups of students must pursue a major research project which culminates in an honors thesis. Library Studies 301H prepares them bibliographically to undertake this task.

Advising for honors and scholars students is done by faculty or by the honors/scholars program staff, who are very supportive of bibliographic instruction. There was little selling to be done, since there was a preexisting market for the course.

COURSE OBJECTIVES

At the end of the course, the student will be able to:

- Understand how scholarly communication patterns influence the structure of information.
- Determine how the bibliography of a discipline reflects existing patterns of scholarly communications.
- Utilize bibliographic resources to solve a research problem.
- Demonstrate mastery of the preceding objectives in a bibliographic research project.

Course Outline

   I. Communication patterns and bibliographic structure in the sciences, social sciences, and humanities
  II. Bibliographic problem solving
 III. Organizing a research project
 IV. Access to internal and external databases
  V. Documenting scholarly research

COURSE REQUIREMENTS

Students are urged to enroll in the course before they initiate their honors research project. There are weekly readings (accompanied by a series of discussion questions) or hands-on exercises using reference sources in the 3 major disciplines. The final bibliographic project consists of 4 parts:

1. A topic definition.
2. A research analysis in which students defend the search strategy they've developed.
3. A properly documented bibliography of approximately 35 to 40 items.
4. An oral presentation which concentrates on the findings presented in the research analysis portion of the paper.

Grades are assigned on the basis of classroom discussion, exercises, and the bibliographic project.

No text is used, simply because a suitable one does not yet exist for this type of course. A list of readings is assigned and discussed in class. Students are encouraged to purchase an appropriate style manual, and some do.

Students are asked to complete a standardized university instructor evaluation form, which collects opinions about the worth of the course and the performance of the instructor. In addition, several informal evaluation discussions are held at various points during the course. The honors program and the scholars program also solicit information about course effectiveness.

STRENGTHS AND WEAKNESSES

The course provides a valuable introduction to scholarly conventions to students having immediate need for this knowledge. It heightens their sensitivity to the potential of the library's resources and to the dynamic role information will play in their scholarly careers. While students appreciate this aspect of Library Studies 301H, they also want basic library instruction—how to use the catalog and indexes, for example. The assumption was made that the honors/scholars student will, perforce, be proficient library users, and this was not the case. The syllabus was not sensitive to this need, and, next fall, the course will open with a 2-week refresher section on basic library skills.

Students were less than enthusiastic about the reading; much of it was assigned in the beginning of the course when students had not yet had a "scholarly experience" to provide a perspective for analysis. The syllabus will be revamped to include this reading later in the semester.

FOR STUDENT READING

Ben-David, J. (1973). How to organize research in the social sciences. *Daedalus, 102,* (2), 39–49.

Eccles, J. (1973). The discipline of science with special reference to the neurosciences. *Daedalus 102,* (2), 85–99.

Fry, N. (1973). The search for acceptable words. *Daedalus, 102,* (2), 11–26.

Garvey, W.P., and Griffith, B. (1971). Scientific communication: Its role in the conduct of research. *American Psychologist, 26,* 349–362. Glueck, W. F., and Jauch, L. (1975). Sources of research ideas among productive scholars. *Journal of Higher Education, 46,* 103–114.

Gombrich, E.H. (1973). Research in the humanities. *Daedalus, 102,* (2), 1–10.

McInnis, R., and MacGregor, J. (1977). Integrating classroom instruction and library research. *Journal of Higher Education, 48,* 17–38.

Raymond, J.C. (1982). Rhetoric: The methodology of the humanities. *College English, 44,* 778–783.

Schwegler, R., and Shamoon, L. (1982). The aims and process of the research paper. *College English, 44,* 817-824.

Skelton, B. (1973). Scientists and social scientists as information users. *Journal of Librarianship, 50,* 138–156.

Stone, S. (1982). Humanities scholars: Information needs and uses. *Journal of Documentation, 38,* 292–313.

Weil, E. (1973). Supporting the humanities. *Daedalus, 102,* 27–38.

Weintraub, K. (1980). Humanistic scholar and the library. *Library Quarterly, 50,*22–39.

Wilson, P. (1980). Limits to the growth of knowledge. *Library Quarterly, 50,* 4–21.

Case Study #11: Pennsylvania State University

University Libraries
University Park, Pennsylvania 16802
Jack Sulzer, Senior Assistant Librarian

Library Studies 470: Federal and Legal Information Resources is a 3-credit course offered annually during the fall semester. Classes meet for 75 minutes twice each week for 15 weeks. Designed primarily for students majoring in political science, the course is also popular with those in law enforcement, history, sociology, and journalism. A minimum of 6 credits in political science, history, or sociology is a prerequisite. Enrollment averages 18 to 20 students, with a maximum number strictly maintained at no more than 25.

The course provides an intensive learning experience for students who anticipate careers in which sources of federal and legal information will be necessary tools. The course also reaches many students who are planning on attending law school. Although political and legal sources are used in other university offerings, none emphasize publication origins, bibliographic access, concepts of information dissemination, or fundamental research techniques.

BACKGROUND

The course was developed and first taught on an experimental basis in 1979 by documents librarians Diane Smith and Susan Anthes. In the fall of 1980, it was permanently added to the Penn State library studies curriculum with the intention of providing an opportunity for graduates, as well as undergraduates, to learn to use a group of specialized resources beyond those covered in the more basic options in the library studies program. The course is presently cotaught by Jack Sulzer and Diane Garner, senior assistant librarian.

Since its inception, the course has changed little. Minor adjustments in content have been necessary, but the only major change has been to reschedule the progression of lectures to accommodate the university's conversion from 10-week terms to 15-week semesters.

Library Studies 470 is team-taught by 2 librarians. As designed, the first third to half of the class covers federal resources. The latter portion concentrates on legal materials and the fundamentals of legal research. Because of this combination of federal and legal research, the course has enjoyed strong support from the political science department since its beginning. Indeed, that department has made Library Studies 470 a de facto prerequisite for their students who plan practicums in public administration or as paralegal assistants.

MARKETING

Originally, the course was advertised through faculty advisors, flyers on bulletin boards in classroom buildings and in the library, and through announcements in various university and student publications. It is now known widely enough that little advertising is necessary beyond announcement in the regular class schedule.

COURSE OBJECTIVES

Upon completion of the course, the student will be able to:

- Interpret bibliographic information for federal and legal documents.
- Develop and complete search strategies in federal and legal documentation through traditional sources.
- Use federal and legal publications as primary information sources in most academic disciplines.
- Know the implications of technological changes on government and legal publications and on the bibliographic access to them.

● Recognize the computerized databases from which government and legal information is available.

Course Outline

I. Introduction to the course; its objectives and requirements
II. Overview of government publications
   A. Depository systems
      1. Government Printing Office
      2. Agency depository systems
   B. Privacy Act
   C. Freedom of Information Act
III. Historical perspective to documents
   A. History of federal publishing
   B. Bibliographic tools for locating historical documents
   Contemporary documents
   A. Bibliographic access to documents
      1. Government Printing Office
      2. Publications: agency
      3. Publications: technical reports
   B. Statistical sources
   C. Executive publications
   D. Legislative research
   E. Judicial publications
   F. Ownership of government information
V. Introduction to legal resources
   A. Basic bibliographic tools
   B. Periodicals
   C. Texts
   D. Restatements
VI. Federal and state statutes and regulations
   A. Statutes
   B. Codifications
   C. Administrative regulations
VII. Courts and their reports
   A. Introduction to court levels
   B. Reporters and Digests
VIII. Citators and their uses
IX. Subject reporting services
X. Computer databases
   A. Basic concepts of computer searching
   B. GPOM, ASI, CIS, NTIS, PTS Federal Index, LEXIS

COURSE REQUIREMENTS

To demonstrate competence in areas within the objectives listed for this course, the student will be required to:

1. Read assigned literature related to the publications of the federal and legal communities.
2. Complete weekly bibliographic and research exercises.
3. Complete a written examination.
4. Complete a comprehensive term research project resulting in a paper which includes: an introduction covering the selection of and approach to the topic; a diary explaining the development and conduct of the search strategy; and an annotated bibliography of primary federal and legal documents on the topic. Students are encouraged to select a topic for which they can write a paper in another course.

TEXT

No text is required for purchase, but students are required to buy a photocopied packet of selected reading materials which include a course bibliography, various research guides, and instructional aids. Other suggested reading material is placed on reserve. No quizzes are given on this material, but students are expected to be familiar with it, particularly as a guide to their research.

EVALUATION

At the end of the course, students complete a standard university evaluation form. This is a machine-readable form which asks the student to rate from "unsatisfactory" to "exceptional" attributes of the course and the instructor, along with overall ratings of both the course and the instructor. Since the course is team-taught, each instructor is rated separately along with that portion of the course. There is also space for written comments on what was liked best and least and suggestions for improvement.

STRENGTHS AND WEAKNESSES

Library Studies 470 has received much positive feedback from its alumni who have gone on to law school or who are working in political or public occupations. It provides not only a fundamental knowledge of federal and legal resources and their use but also good background in general library research. Its greatest advantage is that it gives the student an opportunity to work on a project which is useful in more than one class.

The course does require a great deal of time from both the students and the instructors outside of the classroom. The class research exercises are very time-consuming for the instructors to compose and to grade and for the students to complete. Nevertheless, they are the best possible reinforcement of the classroom work because they provide immediate hands-on experience and are closely tied to the lectures. Although the students complain about them, sometimes bitterly, the only changes that may be made will be to attempt to align them more closely with the research to be done for the term project.

The students also complain about the written examinations, claiming them to be redundant and unnecessary. This, in part, is true. Although the exams are a more objective measurement of a student's understanding of the relationships among the sources than is the completion of a bibliography, they may be changed to shorter quizzes or dropped altogether. They do provide a good barometer of student progress, but they also add to the instructor's burden in preparation and grading.

Since the course is taught in 2 sections, the students tend to segment their learning that way—occasionally to the detriment of their term project. To enhance the correlation between the federal and legal resources, the course is being revised to alternate the 2 parts. For example, lectures on congressional sources and the legislative process will be followed by instruction on the federal statutory materials, finding the laws and tracing their amendments. This will be the first significant change to the outline of the course since its inception. Congressional sources and the legislative process will be followed by instruction on the federal statutory materials, finding the laws and tracing their amendments. This will be the first significant change to the outline of the course since its inception.

Case Study #12: Pennsylvania State University

The University Libraries
University Park, Pennsylvania 16802
Sarah G. W. Kalin, Reference Librarian/
Public Services Coordinator for Online
Catalog
Linda Friend, Coordinator of Database
Search Services

Library Studies 480: Bibliographic Resources and Systems has been offered one semester each year since its inception in 1977. The description in the Penn State catalog is brief and generic: "Survey of information resources, especially computerized bibliographic data files, available from commercial and governmental sources."

It is a 3-credit course designed as an elective, primarily for juniors, seniors, and graduate students in nontechnical majors. The enrollment is limited to a maximum of 15 to preserve the seminar atmosphere. The largest number of students have come from the journalism department (a discipline heavily involved in computerization) and from individuals who plan to go on to graduate library school, although students have also enrolled from such departments as business administration, education, pre-law, and computer science.

BACKGROUND

Library Studies 480 was originally developed in 1977 by Miriam Pierce and Nancy Cline, Penn State librarians, in reaction to the proliferation of online databases and computer technology. Since then, the course has also been taught by Charles G. Murphy, and ourselves. The broad description of this course has allowed considerable latitude in the subjects covered, a highly desirable objective in a subject area as volatile as libraries and information technology. Over the years, the course has evolved into a study of information and its control—past, present, future—with an emphasis on computerization. Promotion of the course has been accomplished by sending signed, personal letters to faculty advisors in selected departments and by posting signs in classroom buildings.

COURSE OBJECTIVES

Upon successful completion of the course, students will be able to:

- Reconstruct the history of information control, recognize some individuals who played a prominent role in this history, and identify the major events that led to the increasing use of information technology.
- Use Penn State's automated catalog and describe its development, implementation, and characteristics.
- Understand the ways in which automation is being applied in libraries and other information centers.
- Recognize the government's role in creating, storing, disseminating, controlling, and manipulating information.
- List ways in which computerized information has been applied in various occupations.
- Given a topic, choose the appropriate databases, construct a simple search strategy, and run the search online to retrieve some relevant materials.
- State ways in which automated information retrieval is affecting daily life, as well as affecting the individual.
- Compare/contrast the ways the public and private sectors manage information.
- Recognize the various techniques (indexing, abstracting, publication, etc.) that are used to control information.
- State ways that the personal computer may be used in information retrieval.

- Project what the future may, or may not, hold as computerization gains momentum.
- Name some of the reasons why information is proliferating at such a rate.

Spring semester 1984 was the first time we prepared a concise list of objectives, and we feel it contributed to our satisfaction with our performance, as well as helping the students to understand why some subject areas were included.

Course Outline

I. Orientation.
II. History of Attempts to Control Information: Brief overview of the ways people have used to organize information, from ancient times to the present.
III. Controlling Information: Technology Comes to the Rescue. Includes proliferation of scientific information; study of Penn State's automated catalog; principles of indexing and abstracting; history of library automation; information networks; the business of computerized information.
IV. Searching Online Databases: After some historical orientation, students learn the basics of computer searching (we used DIALOG's Classroom Instruction Program and the library subsidized an hour of use per student). Students are also exposed to BRS/After Dark.
V. Applications and Effects of Information Technology: Information and the government; economic, social, and cultural problems and issues; computers in the workplace; computer applications in various fields. Demonstration of Kurzweil Reading Machine.
VI. The Future: Is a "Paperless Society" Possible or Desirable? The optimists versus the doomsayers.

COURSE REQUIREMENTS

We use no textbook for this course as an appropriate and acceptable one doesn't appear to exist. Instead, students must make heavy use of reserve readings: *The Guide to Dialog Searching,* professional and popular journal articles, and science fiction.

Examinations include a midterm and final, but various assignments make up most of the grade points. These include construction of a thesaurus on a topic of a student's choice and completion of a worksheet for Penn State's automated catalog, a commentary on the student's online search, a paper on the effects of computerization in a specific field, and an oral presentation on applications of electronic information.

At one time, students were required to hand in a dozen reading cards which were basically summaries of journal articles that the students chose. Because the assignment seemed more of a tedious exercise than a learning experience, it was discontinued. Class participation is also a component of the final grade.

At the conclusion of each course, students fill out Penn State's standard evaluation form, as required by university policy. Each instructor's results are compared universitywide, and the results can be used in preparing promotion and tenure dossiers.

STRENGTHS AND WEAKNESSES

The course basically works well as a nontechnical overview of the "Information Society" for undergraduate and graduate students in many fields and will be a natural for inclusion if and when Penn State defines computer literacy and identifies courses for teaching this elusive concept.

Probably the strongest elements of the course are those we are personally most comfortable with: database searching, history of attempts at controlling information, and library applications of computers. Another strength of Library Studies 480 is its small enrollment, which allows discussion and the development of rapport between students and instructors. Since the classes are composed of upperclassmen, the discussions can be on a fairly high plane. Students consistently report that one of their favorite aspects of the course is the hands-on experience with online searching. Most students spend almost an hour online.

The course has had some difficulty in filling its numbers every year, even though there is a large pool of students from which to draw. The largest registration has been 12 in spite of considerable publicity. "Library Studies" as applied to this course is somewhat misleading since the course is really an introduction to information science and automation (although library applications are included). Cross-listing with a more traditional subject area or a less general course title might give students a better idea of the course content. At one time, the course was a requirement for the Professional Skills Option, a program for doctoral students interested in liberal arts applications of computers but, as of 1984, this option is no longer offered.

COMMENTS

To avoid overburdening one librarian, Library Studies 480 has been team-taught the last 2 times it was offered; team teaching offers the further benefits of sharing ideas and pooling knowledge. The course requires a great deal of outside preparation, since many lectures cover territory that is unfamiliar to librarians. The first time we taught the course, we each received 4 hours released time per week and worked only one night every other week. The second time, we were given no released time.

Preparation time for Library Studies 480 is particularly crucial, since every lecture must be updated to include technological developments over the 12 months since the course was last taught. We estimate that, on average, a 2-hour lecture takes 10 to 20 hours to prepare.

Case Study #13: San Jose State University

Clark Library
San Jose, California 95192-0028
Nancy Emmick, Instructor
Course developed by Judy Reynolds, Nancy Emmick, and Laura Osegueda

San Jose State is the oldest of the 19 California State University campuses. Enrollment for 1984 was 25,000 students, including 7,000 part-time students. Their average age is 29, and the majority commute to campus. The library's holdings include almost 800,000 bound volumes, over 700,000 microforms, and 4,855 current periodical subscriptions. Of the 32 librarians at San Jose, 21 are involved in library instruction.

BACKGROUND

The evolution of this course illustrates the need to work with university departments in order to convince them of the value of library-related courses, as well as exemplifying other problems which arise with library courses. The course developed originally from several discussions between Judy Reynolds, bibliographic instruction program head, and Laura Osegueda, online search services program head, as a way to augment the library's existing instructional programs, which were either geared toward specific subject disciplines or designed as a general introduction for beginning students. The course began as a 2-unit, experimental course to be offered to all interested students, faculty, and the general public. The scope of the course was to be multidisciplinary to allow all majors to benefit. It was initially set up to allow use of the San Jose library school's online laboratory for students who lacked the necessary equipment at home. Knowledge Index, an after-hours version of DIALOG, was selected as the system which the student would access for the majority of the assignments.

After working with the library school dean and the library director, Maureen Pastine, Osegueda was to teach the course in the spring of 1984 with some released time from her library assignment. When she resigned from the university just prior to the beginning of the semester, Nancy Emmick offered to teach the course. However, it was not taught that semester due to insufficient enrollment. It was felt that the course needed more publicity (although fliers were posted throughout the university) as students do not normally scan the course offerings in the School of Library Science, a graduate program.

Emmick, working closely with Pastine, Reynolds, and an academic vice president, arranged for the course to be cross-listed in business as well as library science. The deans of these schools were enthusiastic about this as it allowed FTE'S to be divided between the schools. The course underwent several more changes so that it could be offered through continuing education rather than through the normal curriculum. The course was compacted into 10 sessions rather than the planned 15. The enrollment limit was raised from 15 to 35, therefore restricting some hands-on laboratory sessions. The library school's online laboratory is no longer available, so students will need access to a personal computer or terminal to complete the assignments. The instructor will be working on an overload basis, without released time, but will receive an instructor's fee from the continuing education department. What follows is a description of the newly designed course as it is to be offered.

COURSE OBJECTIVES

The aim of this course is for students to learn how to search databases effectively, using a personal computer or terminal. By the end of the course, students will be expected to be familiar with:

- Computer terminology.
- Database operators.

- Searching techniques and commands.
- Boolean logic.
- Index scope and coverage.
- Available databases.
- Search aids and manuals.
- Current awareness services.

Course Outline

1. Review of objectives, scope, and content of course. Discuss systems.
2. Explanation of telecommunications, computers, terminals, modems, printers, baud requirements, etc.
3. Introduction to Boolean logic, keyword searching, search strategies.
4. Introduce free text searching, the thesaurus, user aids, strings of words.
5. Introduction to Knowledge Index system: commands, selection of databases, search limitations.
6. Introduction to BRS Afterdark: commands, string searching, search limitations.
7. Introduction to The Source and Compuserve: contents and search commands.
8. Introduction to Dow Jones News/Retrieval Service, Information Bank, and Newsnet.
9. Introduction to the Mead systems, computer bulletin boards, teleconferencing, and electronic shopping and banking.
10. Review of final assignment, helpful hints, typical problems, and how to find solutions to problems.

COURSE REQUIREMENTS

- No textbook will be required.
- There will be selected reading assignments in periodicals and textbooks.
- The course will be conducted on a lecture/demonstration/discussion basis.
- Half of the classes will include hands-on exercises of individual database systems.

- There will be no tests, but students will be expected to complete online and offline assignments.
- A final exercise will be the formulation and execution of a search of the student's choice.

Case Study #14: Sangamon State University

Library
Springfield, Illinois 62706
Florence Lewis, Associate Professor of
Library Instructional Services

Sangamon State University is an upper-division, open admissions, public affairs university, located in the capital of Illinois. Its 3,600 students are an average age of 28. Many work full-time, often in state agencies, and attend school at night. The library collection includes 280,000 volumes and 3,000 journal subscriptions. Library literacy continues to be a primary educational goal. Presently, there are 6 librarians on the library faculty, all of whom are involved in library instruction.

COURSE DESCRIPTION

Legal Studies 401: Legal Research and Writing is a required course in the legal studies program. It is team-taught by a member of the library faculty and a member of the legal studies faculty. It carries 4 hours of credit and is open to both undergraduate and graduate students. In this course, students are taught the professional skills needed to research in case, constitutional, statutory, and regulatory law materials and to write legal memoranda. Three sections of the course are offered each year: night courses in both fall and spring, which meet 4 hours once a week, and a day class in the spring which meets for 2 hours twice a week.

BACKGROUND

Legal Studies 401 was the first course offered in the legal studies program, which began in 1977. The library was closely involved in the establishment of the program, and the librarian and legal studies faculty member who first started team-teaching the course also worked together in its development. Since then, 2 additional legal studies faculty members have rotated teaching the course, but the same librarian continues to team-teach with each one.

Even though it is a demanding course, Legal Studies 401 has gained an excellent reputation. As a consequence, it is regularly selected as an elective by students from other university programs.

COURSE OBJECTIVES

By the end of the course, students will be able to:

- Locate legal and other materials in the SSU Library.
- Understand the structure of the U.S. and the Illinois legal systems.
- Understand terms related to legal research.
- Know the basic sources of law in the United States.
- Relate the structure of the U.S. and Illinois legal systems to their literatures.
- Distinguish between primary and secondary sources of the law.
- Identify those publications that are considered primary sources and identify the appropriate finding tools for gaining access to information contained in them.
- Identify the major secondary sources of the law.
- Demonstrate competency in the use of the legal materials presented in the course.
- Develop strategy for solving a given legal problem.
- Distinguish between binding and persuasive authority in law.
- Demonstrate competency in the use of nonlegal materials, both for providing facts and for social policy agreements.
- Demonstrate competency in writing legal memoranda.

Course Outline

    I. Introduction
       A. Course
       B. U.S. legal system
       C. SSU Library and legal collection
   II. Case law reporters
  III. Briefing cases
  IV. Digests and Citators
    V. Memo writing
  VI. Constitutional materials
 VII. Argumentative legal writing
VIII. Legislation (federal and state)
  IX. Administrative law
    X. Using secondary source materials
  XI. Computer-assisted legal research

COURSE REQUIREMENTS

Grades are based upon satisfactory completion of all written assignments and 2 final tests: a take-home writing assignment and an in-class test. Written assignments consist primarily of search problems and legal memoranda. They are due on designated dates and comprise 75 percent of the semester grade.

The take-home examination requires the student to solve a given legal problem through the use of materials presented in the course and accounts for 15 percent of the semester grade. The in-class test consists of 60 multiple-choice questions and makes up 10 percent of the grade.

Required course materials include:

1. Elias, Stephen. (1982). *Legal research.* Berkeley, CA: Nolo Press.
2. *A uniform system of citation.* (1981). (13th ed). Cambridge, MA: Harvard Law Review Association.
3. Statsky, William P., and Wernet, R. John, Jr. (1984). *Case analysis and fundamentals of legal writing.* (2nd ed). St. Paul, MN: West Publishing Co.

At the end of each course, the regular SSU student evaluation form is used to evaluate the course and each instructor. The evaluations are sent directly to the office of the vice president for academic affairs, from which they are processed by the Office of University Research. A computer printout of a summary of the results of each instructor's evaluation is placed in the individual's personnel file.

This course makes heavy demands upon the students, especially in terms of time spent working outside of class. As a consequence, many students have difficulty in completing the course. Those who do successfully complete the course acquire skills which may be profitably applied to future jobs or graduate study.

Students' writing disabilities are quickly revealed in this course. For that reason, the legal studies program recently decided to use this course to demonstrate that students have met the writing competency which is required for graduation. Legal study students who cannot meet the writing requirements dictated by this course are denied credit for the course until they can meet those standards.

Case Study #15: Mankato State University

Memorial Library
Mankato, Minnesota 56001
Sandra K. Ready, Instructional Services
Coordinator

One of 7 publicly supported state universities in Minnesota, Mankato State University enrolls over 13,000 students. The university has an open enrollment policy, accepting over 90 percent of students applying for admission. Most are from Minnesota, with others from surrounding states. The library holds over 650,000 volumes and provides audiovisual materials, maps, government publications, and microforms as well. Of the 20-plus librarians, 2 hold full-time instruction appointments and 8 others participate in integrated classroom instruction.

COURSE DESCRIPTION

Sociology 206: Careers in Criminal Justice is a 4-hour course offered 3 times each year (quarterly). A required course for all corrections majors, it is intended to be taken during the sophomore year. The majority of students enrolling are sophomores or juniors, but some freshmen and seniors usually enroll as well. FTE credits generated by the course are assigned to the sociology department.

Course content is divided into 4 major areas: ethics, professionalism, career exploration, and professional literature and research (referred to as the "library component"). The library component is a 10- to 12-hour module which meets 2 hours weekly, beginning the second or third week of the academic quarter. Since length of quarters fluctuates, specific numbers of class hours and library component content vary. Typically, topics are taught in 2-day units. The first day of each unit is spent in a classroom/lecture setting where specific research tools are introduced and appropriate uses and research methodologies are discussed. The second day is designated as a laboratory day, where students are given an assignment which requires them to use the specific tool discussed to identify library materials relevant to a criminal justice career of their choice.

The library module is a team-teaching endeavor. A librarian is responsible for all instruction; the sociology professor has the responsibility for all grading. Assignment design is a joint activity, and both instructors attend all sessions.

Since the course is a requirement for all corrections majors and must be completed before the students are eligible for internship or field experience, student enrollment has not been a problem. Only one section is offered each quarter, and there is a high demand for space in each section. Every quarter, the course closes before the end of the registration period, with an enrollment of 35 to 40 students.

BACKGROUND

Sociology 206: Careers in Criminal Justice was developed in 1978 to help prepare students entering the field for their work as professionals. At that time, Dr. Linda Saltzman, a sociology professor, was redesigning an existing course to better prepare students in her program for their later coursework and future professional involvement. In discussion with Sandra Ready, a bibliographic instruction librarian, Saltzman determined that a library module would be appropriate. At the librarian's suggestion, the module was designed and inserted into the revised course. Ready and Saltzman have team-taught the library component since its initial offering.

COURSE OBJECTIVES

At the end of the course, the student will:

- Be familiar with the professional and scholarly literature related to the field of criminal justice.
- Be able to select research tools appropriate to a specific topic.
- Be able to find references to library materials using the library's online catalog system.
- Be able to identify Library of Congress subject headings appropriate to a specific topic.
- Be able to select and use indexes and abstracts appropriate to a specific topic.
- Be able to identify and obtain relevant information published by the U.S. government.
- Be able to identify important bibliographic data and to correctly organize a bibliographic citation according to a given style manual.

Course Outline

- I. Introduction to search strategy for criminal justice topics
- II. Using the library catalog; citing monographs
- III. Selecting appropriate indexes and abstracts; obtaining periodical literature; citing articles
- IV. Identifying and obtaining U.S. government publications; citing U.S. publications

COURSE REQUIREMENTS

Students are required to compile a research paper which describes a specific criminal justice career. They must include a job description, necessary education and training, typical responsibilities, salary expectations, and professional organizations and journals relevant to a practitioner in the field. The paper represents approximately 25 percent of the course grade.

Within the library component, students must complete a short assignment dealing with each topic covered. Assignments are evaluated on a "pass-no credit" basis, and "no credit" assignments must be redone if the student wishes credit for the work. Students are encouraged to select topics for each assignment which will produce information they can later incorporate into their research papers.

TEXT

No text is used for the library component. A series of handouts and study guides are used which, when combined with the lectures and classroom experiences, provide the students all necessary information. Since the length and specific content of the module varies from quarter to quarter, both the librarian and the sociology professor have resisted formalizing the materials into a workbook or selecting a specific text.

EVALUATION

Two types of evaluation are used. Students are given a pretest during the first session of the library component and are posttested at the end of the quarter. As might be expected, the majority of students demonstrate increased knowledge of library search strategies and greater familiarity with their professional literature when the scores are compared.

In an attitudinal survey used to evaluate the entire course, students occasionally admit they don't always enjoy the library work, but most express recognition of its value and greater confidence with library work as a result of the library component.

STRENGTHS AND WEAKNESSES

The library component's greatest strength is its direct correlation to student career goals. Since they deal directly with their professional literature, students value the time spent. In addition, the study of search strategy generalizes, so that later, students discover the techniques used in "Careers" can be applied to other courses and disciplines. Frequently, students verbalize this discovery to the librarian or sociology professor.

A primary weakness is the time commitment the librarian must make. The component requires from 10 to 12 hours of classroom instruction each quarter. In addition, preparation and evaluation time are needed. During the 5 or 6 weeks the component meets, the librarian expects to spend 4 to 6 hours weekly dealing primarily with "Careers" materials.

Revision of topics, teaching methods, and assignments has been an ongoing project. As the library changes and as relevant literature in the discipline evolves, the library component must be updated. The 2 instructors do not foresee a time when the library component will no longer need revision.

COMMENTS

At Mankato State's library, there are currently 2 library faculty positions devoted exclusively to instructional services. These librarians have the responsibility for orientation, instruction, production of library handbooks and other publications, and library public relations activities. Since classroom instruction is given first priority, obtaining released time for consultation with cooperating faculty members, lesson planning, and presentation of the library lectures has not been a problem.

In addition to the sociology course, there are 2 credit courses in library skills taught at Mankato State. Both are offered by the library media education department; however, Mankato State librarians are responsible for several sections of each course.

"Library Orientation" is a one-quarter-hour general introduction to library use designed for freshmen and sophomores. It is included in the list of electives available for general education graduation requirements. Since we believe a positive attitude toward the course encourages higher learning outcomes, we librarians have resisted allowing this course to become a graduation requirement.

The second course, "Library Strategies for Graduate Students," is a one-quarter-hour course that stresses the literature relevant to the student's chosen field. At present, this course is an open elective.

A planned course is "Library Orientation II," which will be available to upper-division students and to those who have completed "Library Orientation I." While completion of the first course will not be a prerequisite, students will be encouraged to have done so. The second course will focus on the literature of a specified discipline and will be offered in cooperation with selected departments on campus.

Case Study #16: University of Hawaii–Manoa

**Sinclair Library
Honolulu, Hawaii 96822
Caroline Payne, Reference Librarian**

The University of Hawaii–Manoa, with 21,000 students, is the major comprehensive research campus for the statewide University of Hawaii system. Eighty-two percent of the student body is drawn from the state; however, the university attracts a large number of international students, particularly from Asia. Sinclair Library is the undergraduate library of the university. All 5 librarians are involved in the instructional program as well as in management of the 100,000-volume collection.

COURSE DESCRIPTION

The Library Research Skills Mini-Course, a self-paced program at the University of Hawaii, is offered during fall and spring semesters. Designed as a 5-unit program requiring 5 to 9 hours to complete, the course can be taken for noncredit or can be merged with the requirements of a credit class in the regular university curriculum. Although class level of participants is not restricted, most students represent the undergraduate clientele of the Sinclair Library.

BACKGROUND

The program has evolved through distinct stages. In 1978, Chieko Tachihata, the head of Sinclair Library, and reference librarians Joan Hori, Paula Mochida, and Lucille DeLoach designed a noncredit course consisting of 6 90-minute classes. Believing that library instruction should be offered in various ways to meet the needs of a diverse population, the staff added a self-paced program the following year as an alternative to classroom sessions. Students completed the course at their own pace, but librarians closely followed their progress by grading all assignments.

The first year, 1978–79, 80 students were taught in a formal classroom. Enrollment jumped the following year to 200 in the classroom and 105 in the self-paced option. In part, the leap reflects a textiles faculty member's requirement that her students receive library instruction.

Faced with diminished staffing and a request for instruction for all freshman architecture students, librarians decided to make the program totally self-paced in the fall of 1982. Classroom sessions were abolished; exercises were made self-correcting.

COURSE FORMATS

Presently the program is offered in 2 formats. One format allows students to independently pursue the program without receiving credit. After completing the 5 units, they are offered a final test at the reference desk. In a recent semester, 36 voluntarily enrolled; 3 returned for the test. This may signify that students are not completing the exercises. On the other hand, materials may well provide needed instruction although the student does not return for testing.

In the second format, credit a student receives for the library module is computed in the final grade of a course in the general curriculum. Librarians prepare instructional packets; maintain faculty contact; attend classes, if invited, to introduce the module; assist students with exercises; and keep a permanent record of students completing the program. Faculty distribute packets, give and grade the test, and send permanent records to the library.

MARKETING

Growth of the program has occurred largely through informal faculty contacts. Formal efforts to advertise the program to faculty have not been fruitful. Students are advised of the service through posters, fliers, and notices in the campus papers.

COURSE OBJECTIVES

By completing the program, the student will:

- Become familiar with the variety of library resources in Sinclair Library and Hamilton Library (the graduate and research library).
- Learn techniques used to locate books and periodicals.
- Become familiar with reference materials most commonly used in library research.
- Learn to evaluate library materials and select those most appropriate to his/her needs.
- Learn a systematic method of research for term papers.

Course Outline

Unit 1: Self-guided tour of Sinclair Library
Unit 2: The COM and card catalogs
Unit 3: Periodical indexes and abstracts and newspaper indexes
Unit 4: Reference books
Unit 5: Search strategy

COURSE REQUIREMENTS

For each of the 5 minicourse units, students must read library-prepared descriptions of tools and processes and must subsequently complete a 20-question multiple-choice exercise. Exercises are designed to require interaction with library materials rather than mere rote recall of printed information. After finishing the 5 units, each student takes a 50-question test. Because 3 versions of the final have been developed, a student may retest twice if necessary.

As the course is designed, passing can be defined in 2 ways. The library requires only that the student pass the final test. However, instructors using the minicourse may choose to grade exercises as well.

The self-paced program uses no text but is based on packets prepared by library staff. A packet contains:

- A general course description.
- Five units, each consisting of explanatory guides, an exercise, and an answer key.
- A machine-readable answer sheet.
- A course evaluation form.

Evaluations by students, faculty, and librarians have resulted in course modifications. An evaluation form queries students on level of difficulty, most helpful/least helpful units, and additional coverage desired. Faculty feedback has included test analysis as well as general comments that quality of student papers has improved. Formerly the library used pretests to measure student progress; use was discontinued because few students passed the pretest.

STRENGTHS AND WEAKNESSES

From the library's view, the advantage of the self-paced concept is that it permits a small staff to reach a larger number of students than can be accommodated in classroom sessions. Involving faculty shifts the teaching burden from librarian to teacher; yet standardization of instruction is ensured with the packets. Further, the packet format permits constant revision with minimal difficulty.

From the student's view, flexibility of scheduling is an advantage. In addition, the search strategy-based program imitates the process an undergraduate follows to research and write a term paper.

The minicourse has by no means solidified. During the introductory semester for the self-paced course, assignments were collected from and returned to students at the reference desk; the added burden severely impeded normal reference service. Correcting fill-in-the-blank exercises and keeping records for 200 students with different instructors using different timetables was nightmarish. Now packets are distributed in class, and instructors monitor student progress. The reference desk is the locus for enrollment of students pursuing the program voluntarily, assistance to students having difficulty with exercises, and retesting.

The biggest unsolved problem is lack of control over completion of exercises. Within the staff, there was dispute over supplying answer keys with exercises; the decision to include them was pragmatic, based on staff shortages. Some instructors solved the potential problem of students' using keys to avoid doing exercises by removing keys from their students' packets.

The program functions best when an instructor monitors the completion of each assignment. In a recent semester, fewer than 25 percent of the students in Architecture 100 filled in the exercises; 60 percent passed the examination the first time with 90 percent passing after retesting. If progress is not checked unit by unit, students appear to have a more difficult time passing the test. Presently we are considering offering instructors funds for computer grading to minimize faculty time involvement and improve control over exercise completion.

A program depending solely on printed materials may be disadvantageous for some. Compression of rules and ideas in brief guides results in density of presentation. Some combination of librarian contact, tapes, slides, or computer-assisted instruction along with the packets would be ideal. Earlier, slide-tapes and a videotape were part of the self-paced package; however, students, if unmonitored, bypassed them.

Unless the program is related to a research paper assignment, students may find it boring. Packets have been tailored to student interests by developing a variety of search strategy exercises on drug abuse, social aspects of aging, fashion; now being developed are strategies for education and architecture classes.

Finally, for the program to reach its maximum potential, we want to encourage broader faculty participation. A committed teacher is the strongest factor in the program's success.

Case Study #17: William Paterson College

Sarah Byrd Askew Library
Wayne, New Jersey 07470
Maureen Riley Davis, Instruction Librarian

One of 8 colleges in the New Jersey state system, William Paterson College enrolls 8,500 undergraduate and 1,600 graduate students, most of whom are New Jersey residents and commute to the college. The library resources include over 280,000 books, more than 1,700 periodical titles, and an extensive collection of nonprint media. A "teaching corps" consisting of 9 of the library's 19 professionals, under the direction of a full-time evaluation librarian, is responsible for providing bibliographic instruction.

COURSE DESCRIPTION

The Graduate Education Library Instruction Program (a pilot project) was a multisession module incorporated into ELED609—Research Seminar in Elementary School Subjects, a 3-credit course which met once a week for 2 1/2 hours for 16 weeks. Ten of these sessions were team-taught by the professor, Dr. Mildred Dougherty, and one or more librarians; the remainder of the sessions were taught solely by Dougherty. The length of time devoted to the library instruction component varied from the full period to half, depending on the topic being covered.

BACKGROUND

At the end of the academic year 1979/80, it was observed that 25 percent of the graduate student population had received the traditional "one-shot" instruction that year. In an hour and a half, these sessions could focus attention only on a few major library resources in the field of education. Furthermore, the library instruction staff found itself teaching the same identifiable core curriculum again and again to each of the graduate education classes requesting instruction. Thus, an objective of the instruction librarian for 1980/81 was to find a way to increase the content of instruction given to graduate education students and, at the same time, to eliminate the necessity for teaching the same curriculum repeatedly during the semester.

The possibility of offering a comprehensive library research course to graduate students in education was considered but dismissed because there was no campus mechanism for establishing a course offered by the library faculty. Instead it was decided to demonstrate a need for this type of course and to pilot it in a regularly scheduled graduate research course. Dougherty, an enthusiastic supporter of library instruction, agreed to incorporate the 10 sessions in her seminar and, in 1981, the course was planned.

COURSE OBJECTIVES

At the end of the course, students will have demonstrated a knowledge of the library research process by:

- Selecting and limiting a research topic.
- Developing this topic into a selective bibliography consisting of books, periodical articles, ERIC documents, statistical sources, dissertations, government publications, and other material as pertinent.

Course Outline

    I. Orientation to the WPC Library and its services
    II. Choosing a topic and finding summaries
   III. Narrowing a topic
   IV. Using the card catalog

V.	Finding the best parts of books
VI.	Evaluating books
VII.	Tests and testing
VIII.	Guides to the literature of education
IX.	Collecting current information
X.	Government documents
XI.	Curriculum materials
XII.	Dictionaries, handbooks, directories
XIII.	Other topics—specific to the interests of the students
XIV.	Using other libraries

COURSE REQUIREMENTS

There were no specific assignments but, with each session, students were urged to explore on their own the sources and strategies which were discussed. By the end of the semester, however, students were to have developed a topic suitable for research and a corresponding bibliography.

Library Research Guide to Education, by James R. Kennedy, Jr. (Ann Arbor, MI: Pierian Press, 1979) was the text used to accompany the library instruction units.

Evaluation of the project included a comparison of pre- and posttest results, an evaluative questionnaire completed by the students at the end of the semester, and the personal observations of Dougherty and the librarian.

STRENGTHS AND WEAKNESSES

Presenting the library component in units throughout the semester allowed the students a leisurely pace to familiarize themselves with the tools and gain confidence in their skills. The students were focused and selective in their use of resources and seemed to recognize blind alleys sooner than most.

The team approach and the complete integration of the library component within the research seminar was an ideal medium in which to discuss library strategies and skills. It was, however, somewhat costly when one considers the student/teacher ratio, since at 10 of the sessions both instructors were present, and at 3 of these, they were joined by a second librarian specializing in the topic being discussed. This "visiting specialist" idea was an important element in the design of the library component, never-theless, and allowed students the opportunity to meet librarians in charge of the specialized departments or services they would be using.

One problem with the course outline as presented was the late introduction of indexes and abstracts, which did not occur until the second third of the semester. By this time, several of the students had been guided to sources long before they were discussed in class.

Although this project provided an ideal means to expand the single lecture, it would definitely not reduce the time needed for librarians to teach graduate students. Furthermore, few faculty would be willing to provide this much class time for library instruction. Recommendations were made to reduce and condense the number of units and sessions.

CHANGES

In 1984, a much-modified version of the library instruction module was introduced to students in 5 graduate education research seminars. The program was reduced to 4 units, only the second of which was taught during the regularly scheduled class period. The other 3 2-hour sessions were scheduled at multiple times during the first 2 months of the semester, and students were expected to attend on their own time. The 4 units covered included:

1. Introduction to the WPC library's resources and services and instruction in the use of general education reference materials and indexing and abstracting sources.
2. Reference sources and indexes and abstracts particular to the subject of the seminar, e.g., special education resources and an introduction to computerized database searching.
3. Curriculum materials.
4. Government publications and statistical sources.

PROCEDURES

All students who preregistered for one of the 5 seminars were contacted prior to the beginning of the semester to inform them of the program and the expectation that they attend. Names of the preregistered students were supplied by the registrar, and the college's word processing facilities were used to individualize each letter. Students were asked to select the date they would attend the introductory lecture from 4 dates scheduled and to return an enclosed form to the library. This was a very successful advertising mechanism; 85 percent of the students receiving letters returned forms indicating which date they would attend.

Since this program was developed with and enthusiastically supported by the faculty teaching the seminars, they explained the purpose of the program the first time their classes met and reinforced the attendance requirement. The second unit was scheduled for the time that each faculty member requested it. Announcement of dates for the last 2 units were made during this second session and students again were asked to indicate which of these they would attend.

The concept of the visiting specialist introduced in the pilot was maintained. Each unit was the responsibility of a different librarian, each of whom had expertise or special ability in the area being discussed. The instruction librarian taught only the introductory sessions and did not attend the others.

Although no formal mechanism has been devised for the evaluation of this program, students have responded very favorably and are enthusiastic about it.

Case Study #18: University of California–Irvine

General Library, Reference Department
Irvine, California 92713
Ellen Broidy, Coordinator of Library
Education Services; Social Sciences
Reference Librarian
Chris D. Ferguson, Social Sciences
Bibliographer

The youngest member of the 9-campus University of California system, UCI has 9,400 undergraduates, 1,500 graduate students, and 1,000 medical students and residents. Most undergraduates are from the state with others representing most of the states of the union, and many foreign countries. Undergraduate admission is highly competitive, particularly in technical areas. Graduate admission is competitive across the disciplines.

The 5 UCI libraries hold over a million volumes and nearly 12,000 serial titles. Fifteen of the 47 librarians participate actively in the educational services program.

COURSE DESCRIPTION

Social Sciences 208 is a 2-quarter course offered in the winter and spring quarters. Social Sciences 208A: Thesis Research and Writing covers library-based research and 208B (taught by social sciences faculty) is a writing tutorial. The course is open to graduate students in the School of Social Sciences working toward the M.A., M.A.T., or Ph.D. degrees. It meets weekly for 2 hours throughout the 10-week quarter. Students receive 4 units of credit but no letter grade. Grading is "satisfactory" or "unsatisfactory." The course is an integral part of the graduate program in the School of Social Sciences. Librarians teaching hold adjunct faculty appointments in the school and FTE's are credited to Social Sciences.

BACKGROUND

Social Sciences 208A and 208B were the result of an unplanned meeting of minds. As part of standard faculty liaison activity, the social sciences bibliographer and social sciences reference librarian met with Peter Clecak, the associate dean for graduate studies in the School of Social Sciences. In the course of discussing research difficulties encountered by upper-level graduate students, the idea of offering a course designed to address those problems and the related problem of presentation of the research (writing!) was hatched.

Social Sciences 208A and 208B have been offered 3 times, in 3 slightly different configurations. The first time the course was offered, we planned a one-quarter class, evenly divided between the research and writing components, with the research component team-taught by 2 librarians. This was an overly ambitious undertaking because 5 weeks—half a quarter—simply did not leave enough time to explain and examine the intricacies of library-based research to doctoral students. We looked upon this initial quarter as an experiment.

The response to the concept of the course was uniformly favorable, both from students and instructors, but the attempt to teach the material successfully in one quarter was roundly criticized. In an effort to overcome the perceived deficiencies of a one-quarter course, the instructors proposed a 2-quarter sequence—winter and spring—with the library component falling in the middle and straddling both quarters. Clecak started the course in winter 1983, with a combination of classroom discussions and tutorials. The librarians then took over midwinter quarter. For a myriad of reasons, this arrangement proved unworkable. Students had difficulty making the transition from rather loosely structured discussions about individual writing style to actual classroom presentations. The academic calendar worked against us, with holidays falling on class days, and fewer students appeared after the quarter break.

A comment made by several students who managed to keep track of the class and complete the mixed-up quarter sequence led to a final format change. These students suggested that we simply offer a one-quarter library research course and dispense with the writing component. After consultation with the faculty member, we agreed to keep the course as a 2-quarter sequence, offering the research component in the winter quarter and the writing tutorial, for those desiring it, in the spring.

Social Sciences 208A was offered for the third time in 1984. Due to workload considerations and the fact that the course generally attracts only 8 to 10 students, the coordinator of library education services was the sole instructor of record. If enrollment increases to a point that justifies the time and energy of 2 librarians, we will return to the team-teaching model.

MARKETING

The course benefitted from the early participation of a key faculty member in the School of Social Sciences. Course announcements and syllabi are sent to each graduate student prior to winter quarter preenrollment. Social sciences librarians also have an opportunity to publicize the class during our part of the graduate student orientation each fall.

COURSE OBJECTIVES

The following statement appears on the course syllabus:

"It is expected that participants in this course will gain insights into the methodology of library-based research, the possibilities and limitations of library-based research in the social sciences, the structure of information in the social sciences, and the principal means by which information is generated, stored, transferred and accessed within a given discipline. Participants will acquire:
—generalized knowledge of fundamental bibliographic tools and information sources in the social sciences;
—working knowledge of tools and resources in a particular field of study."

Course Outline

1. Introduction to the course; survey of student interests; library tour.
2. The nature of information—in the social sciences, in the world. The generation and dissemination of knowledge.
3. Basic skills: understanding the library as an information system (or, turning the "invisible college" into the "university of the people"), card catalogs, online catalog.
4. Literature search strategy: guides, handbooks, encyclopedias, directories.
5. Current awareness: indexes, abstracts, citation searching.
6. Government publications.
7. Computer-assisted research: bibliographic and numeric databases, data archives, and data sets.

COURSE REQUIREMENTS

Students enrolled in Social Sciences 208A are required to write a detailed research proposal and produce a 3-part annotated bibliography based upon the research proposal. There are no individual unit assignments.

The bibliography assignment consists of 2 narrative sections and the actual annotated listing. The first section, often lifted from the proposal, is a statement describing the student's current research, emphasizing both descriptive information about the subject (major emphasis, primary hypothesis, basic approach, tentative conclusions) as well as defining the stage of bibliographic inquiry which the student has reached (following a 4-stage model of bibliographic construction: background/overview, preliminary bibliography, extended bibliography, comprehensive bibliography).

The second narrative section, actually following the annotated bibliography, is a search strategy statement. Here we ask the students to describe and evaluate their strategy, addressing such issues as: relative merits and/or drawbacks to *organized* library research, enhanced (or inhibited) control of the literature of the field, and time expended versus tangible rewards gained.

Students are encouraged to limit their project to any aspect of their research that they would think would benefit from bibliographic investigation. A primary goal of the course is that students be able to use the results of this particular academic exercise to either enhance their dissertation research or provide information on sources likely to prove useful when preparing for oral or preliminary examinations.

The actual annotated bibliography is the most mechanistic portion of the assignment. Students are required, insofar as it fits their needs (doctoral students have strange and widely divergent needs), to search for sources in all the types of tools and formats presented in class (encyclopedias, handbooks, card and online catalogs, indexes, microforms, etc.). A computer search subsidy is granted to each student to help offset the cost of an online database search.

There are no required readings for the course. We strongly advise students to familiarize themselves with Carl M. White's *Sources of Information in the Social Sciences* (1973), and, for discussion and argument's sake, the Bath studies on transfer of information in the social sciences (Line, 1971).

EVALUATION

The evaluation mechanism is rather informal. The first year the course was offered, the School of Social Sciences requested that students fill out a standardized evaluation instrument designed for undergraduate courses. We learned little from the responses on that questionnaire. For the past 2 years, we have relied on informal communication with the students, a postcourse discussion with Clecak, and our own written observations on how well we thought the class had gone.

STRENGTHS AND WEAKNESSES

Social sciences graduate students at UCI are, as a rule, relatively sophisticated in terms of their abilities to work in the laboratory or the field. They are far less well-acquainted with the library. Much of what takes place in Social Sciences 208 is remedial. The major strength of the course is its very existence. The fact that key faculty agreed with the library's assessment of the low level of library research sophistication among this particular graduate student population and agreed to support a remedy speaks well for our liaison and cooperative efforts.

The greatest weakness is that students who enroll have widely varying interests and cover the spectrum of research ability from excellent to nonexistent. We are constantly faced with the dilemma of moving too quickly for some while boring others. Ideally, all students entering the class would have minimal exposure to basic library research techniques or at least an understanding of vocabulary, if not concepts. Falling short of that ideal, we struggle along, offering a not-always-successful combination of tools and concepts, stressing the conceptual whenever and wherever possible, but, frankly, running the risk of losing students who view this course as a bandage for a very immediate cut.

REFERENCES

Line, M.B. (1971). *Investigation into information requirements of the social sciences.* (Research Report No. 5). Bath, England: Bath University of Technology.

White, C.W. (1973). *Sources of information in the social sciences, a guide to the literature.* (2nd ed.). Chicago: American Library Association.

Bibliography
Compiled and Annotated by
Sylvia Bender-Lamb

Contained in this bibliography are references to substantive materials regarding credit courses. With few exceptions, all of the references have been published since 1970. Emphasis has been placed on United States sources and examples. Those entries with an asterisk describe courses that appear in the case studies.

PHILOSOPHY OF AND RATIONALE FOR CREDIT COURSES

Beaubien, A.K., Hogan, S.A., and George, M.W. (1982). *Learning the library: Concepts and methods for effective bibliographic instruction.* New York: Bowker.
Excellent overview of pros and cons of library courses in Chapter 10, "Planning Courses." Advocates the "supremacy of the BI course of whatever length over any other mode of instruction."

Dudley, M.S. (1972). Teaching library skills to college students. In M.J. Voight (Ed.), *Advances in librarianship, 3* (pp. 83–105). New York: Seminar Press.
Advocates the credit course as the best solution for undergraduate library instruction.

Eisenbach, E. (1978). Bibliographic instruction from the other side of the desk, *RQ, 17,* 312–316.
Affirms the value for both students and librarians in a bibliographic instruction course at UCLA.

Kennedy, J.R. (1972). Question: A separate course in bibliography or course-related library instruction? In S.H. Lee (Ed.), *Library orientation,* 1st Annual Conference on Library Orien-

Sylvia Bender-Lamb is Coordinator of Instructional Services at the University of the Pacific, Stockton, CA.

tation for Academic Libraries, Ypsilanti, MI, 1971 (pp. 18–28). Ann Arbor, MI: Pierian Press.
Presents both pro and con arguments. Discusses when each method may be appropriate.

Kirkendall, C. (Ed.). (1977). Library instruction: A column of opinion. *Journal of Academic Librarianship, 3,* 94–95.
A variety of answers to the question "Is the undergraduate level general library skills course inefficient and nonrelevant?"

Lester, R. (1979). Why educate the library user? *Aslib Proceedings, 31,* 366–380.
Author argues that formal library instruction courses should be abolished in favor of course-integrated methods.

Morris, J.M. (1980). A philosophical defense of a credit course. In C. Oberman-Soroka (Ed.), *Proceedings from the Second Southeastern Conference on Approaches to Bibliographic Instruction.* Charleston, SC, 1979 (pp. 11–18). Charleston, SC: College of Charleston Library Associates.
Offers a cogent positive position.

INITIATING THE COURSE

Brownson, C.W. (1980). Strategies for promoting library instruction. In C.A. Kirkendall (Ed.), *Reform and renewal in higher education: Implications for library instruction.* 9th Annual Conference on Library Orientation for Academic Libraries, Ypsilanti, MI, 1979 (pp. 73–87). Ann Arbor, MI: Pierian Press.
Presents the political realities of a credit course in terms of curricular innovation.

*Morris, J.M. (1976). Gaining faculty acceptance and support of library instruction: A case study. In H.B. Rader (Ed.), *Faculty involvement in library instruction,* 5th Annual Conference on Library Orientation for Academic Libraries, Ypsilanti, MI, 1975 (pp. 57–73). Ann Arbor, MI: Pierian Press.
Describes the political realities of creating a course in the SUNY College of Environmental Science and Forestry at Syracuse.

Toy, B.M. (1975). *Library instruction at the University of California: Formal courses.* Berkeley, CA: University of California, University Libraries. (ERIC Document Reproduction Service No. ED 116 649)
Stresses the importance of recognizing the library as an academic

department and providing for instruction in library budgets. Gives an overview of problems in starting a formal course.

TEACHING METHODS AND ADMINISTRATION

Biggins, J. (1979). *A study of the administration of library use instruction courses by committee.* Bethesda, MD: ERIC Document Reproduction Service (ED 171 241).
Presents a case study from SUNY Oneonta.

Breivik, P.S. (1982). *Planning the library instruction program.* Chicago: American Library Association.
Discusses the difficulties of offering formal courses. Argues that course-integration, team-teaching, and required instruction offer solutions.

Dudley, M.S. (1977). The state of library instruction credit courses and the state of the use of library skills workbooks. In H.B. Rader (Ed.), *Library instruction in the seventies: State of the art,* 6th Annual Conference on Library Orientation for Academic Libraries, Ypsilanti, MI, 1976 (pp. 79–84). Ann Arbor, MI: Pierian Press.
Supports the self-paced workbook as the only economically feasible method of reaching a significant proportion of the total college and university population.

Hales, C., and Catlett, D. (1984). The credit course: Reaffirmation from two university libraries. Methodology: East Carolina University. *Research Strategies, 2,* 156-165.
Reports on 15 years of evolution in a required course at a state-supported institution of 13,000 students. Includes a lengthy section on problems encountered and modifications made by the instructors, faculty, and graduate students in the Department of Library Science.

*Jacobson, G.N., and Albright, M.J. (1983). Motivation via videotape: Key to undergraduate library instruction in the research library. *Journal of Academic Librarianship, 9,* 270–275.
Indicates significant improvement in attitude toward library and credit course tests at Iowa State University.

Peterschmidt, M.J. (1970). Experiences: Team teaching library instruction at San Jose State College. In *Instruction in the use of the college and university library* (no pagination). Berkeley, CA: University of California, School of Librarianship. (ERIC Document Reproduction Service No. ED 045 103)
Focuses on pros and cons.

Rader, H.B. (1974). Formal courses in bibliography. In J. Lubans, Jr. (Ed.), *Educating the library user* (pp. 279–286). New York: Bowker.

Covers course planning, teaching methods, possible problems, and evaluation. Sample outline of general one-credit course included.

Renford, B., and Hendrickson, L. (1980). *Bibliographic instruction: A handbook.* New York: Neal-Schuman.

Chapter 5 focuses on workbooks with attention to obstacles in using workbooks in credit courses. Chapter 6 summarizes prevailing pro and con arguments on separate courses and offers specific guidance on implementing, teaching, and promoting credit courses.

Richardson, L.L. (1984). Teaching basic library skills: Past tense, future perfect. *RSR: Reference Services Review, 12,* (1), 67–76.

Discusses comprehensive self-instruction as a flexible alternative to self-paced workbooks in credit courses.

Roberts, A.F. (1982). *Library instruction for librarians.* Littleton, CO: Libraries Unlimited.

Information on courses in the "Methods of Library Instruction" chapter includes outlines for both a basic and an advanced course.

Tucker, E.E. (1974). *A study of the effects of using professional library staff as coinstructors in an instructional program.* (Doctoral dissertation, Florida State University).

Compares student learning in basic library use class taught by librarians versus regular instructors.

EVALUATION OF CREDIT COURSES

Eyman, D.H., and Nunley, A.C., Jr. (1978). *The effectiveness of Library Science 1011 in teaching bibliographic skills.* Tahlequah, OK: Northeastern Oklahoma State University. (ERIC Document Reproduction Service No. ED 150 962)

Compares acquisition of library skills (as demonstrated by the ability to interpret parts of a catalog card and index entries) for students enrolled in credit course with group not taking course. Recommends course-related instruction rather than credit course since no advantage was discovered.

McQuistion, V.F. (1984). The credit course: Reaffirmation from two university libraries. Measurement: Millikin University. *Research Strategies, 2,* 166-171.

Reports significantly positive results in upgrading students' ability to design research strategies and use resources effectively through a required course at this 1,500-student institution. Focus is on a pre- and posttest evaluation methodology, although other measures were also utilized by the instructors.

Person, R. (1981). Long-term evaluation of bibliographic instruction: Lasting encouragement. *College and Research Libraries, 42,* 19–25.
Survey of students who had previously taken library skills course at Southern Illinois University. Results indicated high value for the course and increased confidence in using libraries. Conclusions marred by low response rate to survey.

Reeves, P. (1979). *Library services for non-traditional students. Final report.* Ypsilanti, MI: Eastern Michigan University. (ERIC Document Reproduction Service No. ED 184 550)
Test results revealed an improvement in library skills among those taking course, no significant variation between nontraditional students and others succeeding with course, and no significant effect in courses taken concurrently.

Selegean, J.C., Thomas, M.L., and Richman, M.L. (1983). Long-range effectiveness of library use instruction. *College and Research Libraries, 44,* 476–480.
Gives a credit course emphasis.

Stewart, B.C. (1976). *An evaluation of a course in library instruction at Ball State University.* Bethesda, MD: ERIC Document Reproduction Service (ED 138 246).
Found significant benefit obtained from formal library instruction course.

Sugrañes, M.R., and Neal, J.A. (1983). Evaluation of a self-paced bibliographic instruction course. *College and Research Libraries, 44,* 444–457.
Discusses procedures for evaluating instructional effectiveness of materials and methods used in a California State University–Long Beach course.

Wood, R.J. (1984). The impact of a library research course on students at Slippery Rock University. *Journal of Academic Librarianship, 10,* 278–284.
Suggests a significant positive gain in both knowledge and attitude.

COURSE DESCRIPTIONS AND CONTENT: GENERAL

Blum, M.E., and Spangehl, S. (1977, November). *Introducing the college student to academic inquiry: An individualized course in library research.* Paper presented at the International Congress for Individualized Instruction, Lafayette, IN. (ERIC

Document Reproduction Service No. ED 152 315)
Critical thinking is among the topics covered. Includes course materials.

DeHart, F.E. (1974). *The library-college concept: For the want of a horse shoe nail.* Emporia, KS: Kansas State Teachers College, Graduate Library School. (ERIC Document Reproduction Service No. ED 098 995)
Describes an upper-division course taught cooperatively by librarians and teaching faculty.

Droog, J. (1976). The education of the information user. *International Forum on Information and Documentation, 1,* 26–32.
Describes pilot project to develop a course.

Dunlap, C.R. (1976). Library services to the graduate community: The University of Michigan. *College and Research Libraries, 37,* 247–251.
Supports separate, full-term graduate-level courses.

Kibby, R.A., and Weiner, A.M. (1983). U.S.F. Library lectures, revisited. *RQ, 13,* 139–142.
Describes format and content of undergraduate class, textbook, and lectures. Includes comments on evaluation.

Krzywkowski, V.I. (1983, April). Bibliographic instruction for undergraduate students: Development of a one credit course. In E.A. Franco (Ed.), *Improving the use of libraries.* Proceedings from the spring meeting of the Nebraska Library Association, College and University Section, Peru, Nebraska. Bethesda, MD: ERIC Document Reproduction Service (ED 234 817).
Case study from Kearney State College, Nebraska.

Oberman-Soroka, C. (1980). *Petals around a rose: Abstract reasoning and bibliographic instruction.* Chicago: Association of College and Research Libraries.
Discusses an undergraduate course at the College of Charleston centered on analysis, linkage, and evaluation in the teaching of bibliographic instruction.

Rettig, J. (1977). General library skills credit courses. In T. Kirk (Ed.), *State-of-the-art of academic library instruction. 1977 update* (pp. 79–113). Chicago: American Library Association. (ERIC Document Reproduction Service No. ED 171 272)
Updates Robison (1973) report.

Roberts, A. (1978). *A study of 10 SUNY campuses offering an undergraduate credit course in library instruction.* Albany, NY: State University of New York, University Libraries. (ERIC Document Reproduction Service No. ED 157 529)

Includes material on the personality of the instruction librarian as a factor in bibliographic instruction.

Robison, D. (1973). Institutions offering a formal course with or without credit. In T. Kirk (Ed.), *Academic library bibliographic instruction: Status report 1972* (pp. 8–18). Chicago: Association of College and Research Libraries. (ERIC Document Reproduction Service No. ED 072 823)
Survey of programs, noting long-standing examples and norms for credit course instruction.

*Shain, C. (1970). Bibliography I: The UC Berkeley experience. In *Instruction in the use of the college and university library* (no pagination). Berkeley, CA: University of California, School of Librarianship. (ERIC Document Reproduction Service No. ED 045 103)
Discusses content and evolution, growth and administrative problems, and the future.

*Smalley, T.N. (1983). *Bibliographic instruction for undergraduates. An example of one-unit required library skills course.* Plattsburgh, NY: State University of New York. (ERIC Document Reproduction Service No. ED 232 656)
Presented within the context of 2 conceptual structures: principles underlying information access systems and the distinctive discipline contexts of the research process. Extensive appendices of course materials.

Stillerman, S.J. (1975). *Format for library instruction: Stated student preferences at a community college.* Bethesda, MD: ERIC Document Reproduction Service (ED 115 294).
Despite exposure to library orientation in English classes, survey revealed most students are still deficient in research skills. Proposes a course to remedy situation.

White, E. (1977). Course related bibliographic instruction for credit. In T. Kirk (Ed.), *State-of-the-art of academic library instruction. 1977 update* (pp. 114–127). Chicago: American Library Association. (ERIC Document Reproduction Service No. ED 171 272)
Continues and expands on Robison (1973). Title listed in table of contents is "Upper-level subject related credit courses."

COURSE MATERIALS: GENERAL

Adalian, P.T., and Rockman, I.F. (1981). *BLISS: Basic library information sources and strategies: A handbook for Library 101.* San Luis Obispo, CA: California Polytechnic State University. (ERIC Document Reproduction Service No. ED 200 202)

Support manual for class lectures.

Bhullar, P., and Hosel, H.V. (Eds.). (1979). *Library skills.* Columbia, MO: University of Missouri, School of Library and Information Science. (ERIC Document Reproduction Service No. ED 190 083)

Text designed for use at the University of Missouri.

Bodien, C., and Smith, M.K. (1978). *Developing library skills: How to use the university library.* Bemidji, MN: Bemidji State University, A.C. Clark Library. (ERIC Document Reproduction Service No. ED 153 656)

Text for a one-credit course.

Clement, R.T., et al. (1981). *Using the Joseph F. Smith Library.* Laie, HI: Brigham Young University–Hawaii, Joseph F. Smith Library. (ERIC Document Reproduction Service No. ED 201 328)

Syllabus for 2-credit required course, taught jointly by librarians and English faculty.

Els, P., and Amen, K.L. (1978). *Introduction to bibliography.* San Antonio, TX: St. Mary's University. (ERIC Document Reproduction Service No. ED 156 107)

Text for credit course.

Gavryck, J., et al. (1981). *Library research curriculum materials for a one-credit course.* Albany, NY: State University of New York. (ERIC Document Reproduction Service No. ED 203 884)

Gives a course outline, objectives, pretest, exercises, and 10 units for an undergraduate course.

Gebhard, P. (1979). *Library research: A beginning text in bibliographic searching.* Santa Barbara, CA: University of California, University Library. (ERIC Document Reproduction Service No. 167 134)

Manual used in 2-credit, upper-division course. Assignments designed to promote critical thinking and problem-solving skills.

Gebhard, P., and Silver, B. (1978). *Library skills: A self-paced workbook.* Santa Barbara, CA: University of California, University Library. (ERIC Document Reproduction Service ED 167 133)

One-unit course for freshmen and incoming students.

*Huston, M., and Robinson, D.M. (1981). *Library research source curricular package.* Bethesda, MD: ERIC Document Reproduction Service (ED 213 416).
A course designed to teach basic skills in a conceptual framework at Evergreen State College, Washington.

*Johnson, B.L. (1976). *Methods of library use: Handbook for Bibliography I.* Berkeley, CA: University of California, School of Librarianship. (ERIC Document Reproduction Service No. ED 129 340)
General text for Berkeley's undergraduate course.

Morrison, R.L., and Nollen, T. (1982). *Library skills workbook. First edition.* Bethesda, MD: ERIC Document Reproduction Service (ED 233 726).
A self-instructional workbook for Pittsburgh State University, Kansas, undergraduate students. Required in a composition course.

Rice, S. (1979). *Workbook for the introduction to the library.* Ann Arbor, MI: University of Michigan, University Libraries. (ERIC Document Reproduction Service No. ED 163 953)
Undergraduate library workbook.

Rominger, C.A. (Ed.). (1975). *Handbook for English 48: Introduction to library research and bibliography.* Davis, CA: University of California, University Library (ERIC Document Reproduction Service No. ED 108 670)
The course includes 8 lectures, practical assignments, and a term project.

COURSE DESCRIPTIONS AND CONTENT: SUBJECT

Johnson, P.T. (1974). The Latin American subject specialist and bibliographic instruction. In *Seminar on the Acquisition of Latin American Library Materials, Final Report and Working Papers, 19,* 203–221.
Describes a discipline-based course, compilation of a literature guide for use as a text, materials to be covered, and exercises.

Jones, G. (1973). Using the chemical literature—An undergraduate course? *Education in Chemistry, 10,* 11.
Describes a course offered only once because of difficulties encountered in carrying out the actual searches.

Lee, J.W., and Read, R.L. (1973). Making the library good for business. *Learning Today, 6* (2), 36–41.

Seventy-seven percent of postgraduate business students surveyed favored a formal course in library use.

Lowry, G.R. (1980, March). *Online document retrieval system education for undergraduates: Rationale, content, and observations.* Paper presented at the National Online Information Meeting, New York, NY. (ERIC Document Reproduction Service No. ED 183 176)
Discusses a course in online skills at Stockton State College, New Jersey.

Lunin, L.F., and Catlin, F.I. (1970). Information science in the medical school curriculum: A pioneer effort. In J.B. North (Ed.), *Information Conscious Society, Vol. 7* (pp. 37–39). Washington, DC: American Society of Information Scientists.
Describes a 10-week course at Johns Hopkins utilizing video lectures and tutorials to teach searching, evaluating, and retrieving skills in biomedicine.

Martin, J., House, D.L., Jr., and Chandler, H.R. (1975). Teaching of formal courses by medical librarians. *Journal of Medical Education, 50,* 883–887.
Describes several courses at the University of Tennessee Center for Health Sciences.

Nettlefold, B.A. (1975). A course in communication and information retrieval for undergraduate biologists. *Journal of Biological Education, 9,* 201–205.
Required course taught by librarians at Paisley College of Technology in Pennsylvania.

*Osegueda, L., and Reynolds, J. (1982). Introducing online skills into the university curriculum. *RQ, 22,* 10–11.
Proposes a pass/fail credit course covering DIALOG, BRS, basic search strategy, and Boolean logic for undergraduates and community members at San Jose State University, California.

Paugh, S.L., and Marco, G.A. (1973). Music bibliography course: Status and quo. *Music Library Association Notes, 30,* 260–262.
Presents a survey of courses. Authors recommend broader approach and more stimulating teaching methods.

Shearer, B., et al. (1980). *Bibliographic instruction through the Related Studies Division in vocational education: LRC guide, pathfinders, and script for slide presentation.* Bethesda, MD: ERIC Document Reproduction Service (ED 205 171).
Describes course offered at Tri-Cities State Technical Institute in Tennessee.

Ramsay, O.B. (1976). Individualized instruction and evaluation of users in the chemical literature. In H.B. Rader (Ed.), *Faculty involvement in library instruction,* 5th Annual Conference on Library Orientation for Academic Libraries, Ypsilanti, MI, 1975 (pp. 43–55). Ann Arbor, MI: Pierian Press.

A survey of trends in chemical course offerings.

Walser, K.P., and Kruse, K.W. (1977). A college course for nurses on the utilization of library resources. *Medical Library Association Bulletin, 65,* 265–267.

Describes a 10-week, one-and-a-half credit required course for undergraduates.

Will, L.D. (1972). Finding information: A course for physics students. *Physics Bulletin, 23,* 539–540.

Describes a 2-phase program for first- and second-year students, utilizing a project and self-learning methods.

COURSE MATERIALS: SUBJECT

Bryson, E.M., and Kelly, W. (1982). *Library research manual: History.* Bethesda, MD: ERIC Document Reproduction Service (ED 229 011).

Cooperatively administered workbook in western civilization.

Hodina, A., et al. (1981). *Information resources in the sciences and engineering: A laboratory workbook.* Santa Barbara, CA: University of California, University Library. (ERIC Document Reproduction Service No. 205 178)

Designed for upper-level undergraduates and graduates, covering print and online sources.

Pikoff, H. (1978). *Workbook for library research in psychology.* Bethesda, MD: ERIC Document Reproduction Service (ED 151 025).

SUNY–Buffalo product designed for wider use.

Smalley, T.N. (1978). *Basic reference tools for nursing research: A workbook with explanation and examples.* Plattsburgh, NY: State University of New York. (ERIC Document Reproduction Service No. ED 197 071)

Covers medicine, nursing, and allied health fields.

COURSE DESCRIPTIONS AND CONTENT: SPECIAL GROUPS

Dudley, M.S. (1970). *Chicano library project, based on the "Research skills in the library context" program developed for Chicano high potential students in the Department of Special Education Programs.* (UCLA Occasional Paper, No. 17) Los Angeles: University of California, University Library. (ERIC Document Reproduction Service No. ED 045 105).

Describes a self-paced course in undergraduate library skills using the original workbook concept.

Library skills course for EOP students. (1981). Plattsburgh, NY: State University of New York. (ERIC Document Reproduction Service No. ED 202 459)

Describes a 5-week course offered the summer before a student's first semester.

Palmer, V.E. (1982). B.I. for the invisible university. *College and Research Libraries News, 43,* 12–13.

Course targeted at independent and nonaffiliated learners at Miami University, Ohio.

Rockman, I.F. (1978). *Library instruction to EOP students: A case study.* Bethesda, MD: ERIC Document Reproduction Service (ED 174 211).

Describes a 10-week required one-unit course at California Polytechnic State University–San Luis Obispo.

Other Resources

Following is a list of materials which as of this writing are commercially available. Prices, always subject to change, are given primarily for purposes of comparison.

TEXTBOOKS

For Use with Students in All Majors

Cook, M.G. (1975). *The new library key.* (3rd ed.). New York: H. W. Wilson. $7.
> Begins with chapters on libraries, books, and catalogs and classification. A chapter on writing the research paper is followed by chapters on general sources: encyclopedias, dictionaries, periodical indexes, and general reference. The next 6 chapters deal with reference books in various subject areas, along with another on nonbook materials.
>
> First published in 1956, this book contains many examples and situations that date back to its first edition. Somewhat of a search strategy is reflected in its organization, and examples of note-taking appear throughout the chapters. There are copious annotations of reference materials, but these are now 10 years old.

Gates, J.K. (1983). *Guide to the use of libraries and information sources.* (5th ed.). New York: McGraw-Hill. $19.95; $13.95 (paper).
> Perhaps the most widely used text for library courses which use commercial texts. It begins with a section on books and libraries, followed by a section on the organization and arrangement of library materials. The next 2 sections, the larger part of the book, are lengthy discussions and annotations of general reference materials and reference materials in subject fields. The latest edition includes a chapter on nonprint information sources and a short section on online searching. The book ends with a brief chapter on researching a paper in the library. This is a good compendium of materials in various subject areas, written in a clear and formal style. However, its lack of emphasis on process limits its use in courses that are designed to teach strategies for locating information. In addition, most students would use only the sections in the book that apply to their topics and may resent paying a rather hefty price.

Hauer, W.G., et al. (1983). *Books, libraries, and research.* (2nd ed.). Dubuque, IA: Kendall/Hunt. $11.95 (paper).

Begins with background on books, libraries, and different formats of library materials, followed by chapters on the research paper, classification, card catalog, reference books, indexes, and government publications. Each chapter ends with review questions and most with a worksheet. Pages are perforated for easy tear-out.

The arrangement lends itself more easily than other books to teaching a search strategy approach. Brief discussions of both computerized cataloging and online searching and catalogs are included. It is clearly written. Assignments are adequate, with an emphasis on tool usage.

Katz, W. (1979). *Your library: A reference guide.* New York: Holt, Rinehart and Winston. $19.95; $10.50 (paper).

Although the stated purpose of this book is to serve as an introduction for anyone beginning to use a library, it is really a guide to reference sources for a layperson. The first section discusses how to make good use of a library and reference works, while the second section, arranged by discipline, provides guides to the literature for these disciplines.

The book is written in an informal and interesting style. Of particular use are the flowcharts for each discipline, which help the reader to analyze his/her question and go to the appropriate source. The book could serve as a text for a course organized around finding different types of information.

Lolley, J.L. (1974). *Your library—What's in it for you?* New York: Wiley. $5.95 (paper).

Designed as a self-instructional guide, this book combines text and accompanying exercises. There are sections on the library catalog, periodicals, and reference books. The section on library services asks students to locate and find out about such things as browsing books, typewriters, college catalogs, reserve room, and librarians. The final chapter is on writing a research paper.

The writing style is sprightly and entertaining, and there are also cartoons and photographs from old movies to make the format even more lively. Exercises are mostly fill-in-the-blank, and an answer key is included. This book is probably a better choice than many locally produced workbooks (students will actually read it), but again its lack of emphasis on strategy limits its use in many courses. Its modest price is also an asset. Its age is not.

Walsh, P., and Giessen, H. (1983). *Research in practice: A workbook for the college student.* Redding Ridge, CT: Professional Services Publishing Co. $17.50 (paper).

A workbook used in a one-credit research skills course required for freshmen at the University of Bridgeport. Contains many exercises, including card catalog use, government documents, and the research process.

Wolf, C.E., and Wolf, R. (1981). *Basic library skills: A short course.* Jefferson, NC: McFarland and Co. $8.95 (paper).

This text is designed for either self-instructional use or for a library course in basic skills. It is organized with a chapter on getting acquainted with the library, followed by chapters on the card catalog, bibliographies, and others on types of reference works, with annotations. The final chapter contains hints for writing papers. Each chapter begins with objectives and ends with questions, whose answers are in the back of the book. It is presented in an unexciting format and style, but it is clearly written. Although recent, there is no mention of database searching or search strategies.

For Use with Students in Certain Majors

*Library research guide to . . .*Ann Arbor, MI: Pierian Press. $17.95; $9.95 (paper).

Titles are currently available on biology, education, history, music, psychology, religion and theology, and sociology. These are aimed at upper-level students who have a knowledge of basic library tools such as the card catalog and the *Readers' Guide.* Each volume is organized according to search strategy: typical chapters are topic selection, narrowing a topic, locating books, evaluating books, collecting current information, using guides to the literature, and using other libraries. Special topics of interest to the discipline are included (tests for education, review serials for biology, biography for history, statistics for sociology, etc.).

Each title has a separate author and reflects that author's style, but they all tend to be well-written with copious examples of research problems in each discipline. For courses emphasizing a search strategy approach and planned for specific majors, this series may work well. It could also be effective for courses serving many majors. Ordering a few copies of each title for the bookstore may be mechanically unwieldy, but the series could easily be available on reserve.

One drawback is the poor design of the books. They are oversized with narrow margins, and reproductions of index entries, etc., tend to be poor. The format improves with volumes published later.

*Materials and methods for . . .*New York: Neal-Schuman. Instructor's manual $21.95; workbooks $7 each for 5 or more.

Included are titles on business, history, political science, and sociology. This series is designed to be used as workbooks by students in a particular discipline. The instructor's manual includes 20 sets of "fill-ins" so that the exercises require different answers. The text is organized around types of literature in the discipline: guides to the literature, handbooks, yearbook, dictionaries and encyclopedias, indexes and abstracts, bibliographies, scholarly journals. There is a chapter on book evaluation, as well as one on research paper methodology. Each chapter is followed by a worksheet.

The textual information tends to be brief, with an emphasis on the annotation of tools. The worksheets concentrate on asking students to fill in information located in a library tool. Titles from the series might be used for courses for majors, to teach the mechanics of using various tools. They might also be valuable as workbooks to accompany a nonlibrary course with a library component. Since multiple sets are already arranged for, and answers provided, using this series could save hours of librarian time.

Two texts, which are currently out of print but which are worth looking at for their teaching ideas and examples, are:

Gore, Daniel. (1968). *Bibliography for beginners: Form A.* New York: Appleton-Century Crofts.

Morris, Jacquelyn, and Elkins, Elizabeth A. (1978). *Library searching: Resources and strategies with examples from the environmental sciences.* New York: Jeffrey Norton.

For Additional Ideas

There are also available various guides to research, written for particular disciplines. Most have only a chapter on library use, and these often contain glaring errors and omissions. Examine them carefully. Two which were coauthored by librarians are:

Kartis, Alexia M., and Watters, Annette Jones. (1983). *Library research strategies for educators.* (PDK Fastback #192). Bloomington, IN: Phi Delta Kappa. Price not available.

While this is actually a pamphlet, it contains up-to-date information written more from a researcher's point of view than a librarian's.

Reed, Jeffrey G., and Baxter, Pam M. (1983). *Library use: A handbook for psychology.* Washington, DC: American Psychological Association. $15 (paper).

This book contains sound discussions on topic selection, computer searching, and interlibrary loans.

STYLE MANUALS

In many library courses, students are asked to purchase a style manual rather than a text. Although these manuals do not contain information on library research, they do include bibliographic format and directions for the typing and layout of research papers. Students may consider them a worthwhile purchase for future use (and they may be a required purchase for other classes). Those listed below are the most commonly used:

American Psychological Association. (1983). *Publication manual of the American Psychological Association.* (3rd ed.). Washington, DC: American Psychological Association. $15 (paper).

Gibaldi, Joseph, and Achtert, Walter S. (1980). *MLA handbook for writers of research papers, theses and dissertations.* (Student edition). New York: Modern Language Association. $9.50; $6.75 (paper).

Turabian, Kate. (1977). *A manual for writers of term papers, theses, and dissertations.* (4th ed.). Chicago: University of Chicago Press. $14; $4.50 (paper).

Turabian, Kate. (1977). *Student's guide for writing college papers.* (3rd rev. ed.). Chicago: University of Chicago Press. $14; $4.50 (paper).

AUDIOVISUAL MATERIALS

For college library instruction, there are few commercially prepared audiovisual materials which are of acceptable quality and level. One producer which has good materials is:

Oak Woods Media, 2243 South 11th Street, Kalamazoo, MI 49009. Six slide/tapes on indexes: *Readers' Guide, Business Periodicals Index, Education Index, Humanities Index, Social Sciences Index,* and *Essay and General Literature Index.*

Six slide/tapes on ERIC: Orientation, *RIE, CIJE, AIM/ARM, Resources in Vocational Education* and *Exceptional Child Education Resources.*

Each slide/tape is $75. No preview is available, but materials may be returned within 30 days after purchase.

Appendix: Tricks of the Trade

Any experienced teacher develops techniques which help in classroom management and solving (or presenting) day-to-day problems. Following is a potpourri of tips and tricks, gathered from good teachers in several disciplines over a number of years.

SETTING THE STAGE ON THE FIRST DAY

The first day of class sets the stage for the rest of the semester. It's on this day that students decide whether the course is going to be serious or trivial, easy or difficult. The attitude of the teacher is all-important. One librarian stated in a group meeting that she was honest and "up front" with her students, telling them right at the beginning that the subject matter was boring. Chances are she convinced all her students that it was.

One good teacher asks his students on the first day of class to list behaviors of the worst teachers they've had. With relish, they castigate instructors who hand back assignments late, aren't prepared, come to class late or not at all, test on materials not covered, ridicule students, etc. The teacher then asks what students do which teachers consider to be bad behavior and, of course, the lists are very similar. He tells the students he won't do the things on the list if they won't—and that way they'll all win.

A special problem with library courses is that students may have chosen the class because they think it's easy. If the course is demanding, as it should be, the first day is the time to make these expectations clear.

BREAKING THE ICE

In classes on small campuses, or ones made up of the same majors, many of the students may already know each other. Library courses often, however, draw students from all over the campus who are as new to each other as to the instructor. If the class is under 40, having students introduce themselves helps to create a better feeling in the class.

Unlike librarians at a professional meeting, students at this point will not volunteer a great deal of information. In order to avoid their merely mumbling names and majors, begin with a self-introduction and then ask who'd like to be next. Those who are least shy and most talkative will be the first to volunteer. Make reinforcing comments as students give interesting responses ("that sounds like an intriguing career choice").

GETTING TO KNOW STUDENTS' NAMES

We all like to have our names remembered. Students are pleased and appreciative when the teacher knows them early in the semester. Take attendance on something large enough to write comments ("curly hair, nice smile"). If it's a very large class, have a seating chart and ask students to sit in the same place each time. During the pretest is a good time to practice going over the names and matching them with the descriptions.

ENCOURAGING ATTENDANCE

The easiest way to encourage attendance is to require it. Many faculty, especially those who were students in the 60s, feel uncomfortable requiring attendance: after all, if the coursework is truly valuable, won't students attend of their own volition? Other teachers feel that students should be guided, perhaps even forced, to do what is best for themselves.

If you don't require attendance (yet still want students to come to class sessions), you should make clear that attendance is expected. Ask students who were absent at the last class session if they've been ill, and tell them they were missed. If the instructor ever intimates that attendance is not important, the students will take this as their guide.

STARTING CLASS PROMPTLY

If it isn't, the students won't be.

DISTRIBUTING MATERIALS

It's tempting to pass out the entire day's worth of handouts right at the beginning of the period. Don't. Students will look at them then instead of paying attention to you. Distribute each handout just before it's to be discussed.

COLLECTING MATERIALS

If assignments aren't collected until the end of the period, students will complete last week's assignment in this week's class.

LETTING OTHER LIBRARIANS KNOW ABOUT ASSIGNMENTS

Support from the rest of the library staff is crucial to the success of the course. If they're asked questions they can't answer, they may feel ignorant. Some library course instructors have put together notebooks to leave at the reference desk, complete with finished assignments and notes as to how much help their students should have. Others circulate a memo of explanation at the beginning of each course or as each unit starts. Certainly, before one assignment creates a run on specific reference books or library area, the person in charge of that area should be warned.

PROMPT TURN-AROUND TIME ON ASSIGNMENTS

Students want prompt feedback on their work, and it's more effective when it's sooner. Don't put off doing the grading.

CHECKING STUDENT SPELLING

One librarian reports that her student, who was working on a topic unfamiliar to her, spent half the course without finding materials on his topic. He'd spelled it wrong.

DISCOURAGING CHEATING

Unfortunately, cheating is prevalent on college campuses. To discourage cheating, keep multiple-choice testing to a minimum; never give the same multiple-choice test 2 terms in a row. If the order of the questions varies, and the students do not keep the exam, then the same questions can be reused.

Separate and scatter students when they take a test. One teacher, who has very large sections meeting in a relatively small room, runs his test off on different colored paper. The student sitting next to someone with a blue sheet thinks his yellow sheet is a different test.

Stand up and move around the room while a test is being administered. Students will also be more willing to ask questions of a teacher who is on his/her feet. Also, avoid giving assignments semester after semester which ask the same questions, to be answered in the same way, of everyone.

KEEPING STUDENTS INFORMED

Students need to know ahead of time what will be happening in class. Major dates, such as midterm or final examinations or the due date of a class project, should probably be announced on the syllabus. Some good instructors are so organized that each class's topic as well as each assignment's due date is listed on the syllabus (and this is certainly feasible if the class meets up to only 10 or 15 times). Other instructors like to have more flexibility, but even so, students should know what's planned for the next 2 or 3 class periods. Students seldom forgive the instructor who suddenly assigns a paper or major examination on a week's notice.

DEALING WITH DISCIPLINE

College classes seldom exhibit the same kinds of disruptive behavior which high school classes do. However, there may sometimes be students who behave rudely. They may be passive resisters who read a newspaper in class or whose very evident body posture emanates boredom and resentment. Some students may make rude remarks. These behaviors are most likely to occur in a required class from students who do not want to be there.

Many of these problems can be avoided by setting a serious and concerned tone from the first day of class and by giving a number of examples of the usefulness of the course. If problems do occur, do not comment in front of the entire group; the situation may quickly escalate into a no-win confrontation.

Quietly ask the student to talk to you after class (if possible, in your office or another private place). Tell the student that his/her conduct is annoying, and ask directly why s/he is behaving in such a nonadult manner. It's possible that student has other problems which are interfering with the class. Discussing the obtrusive behavior may not change the student's attitude but, almost always, the behavior will cease being so overt.

Even the very best instructors will occasionally have a class that never quite seems to gel. Make it through the semester by keeping the class on a professional and serious level.

Index

Compiled by Linda Webster